*impromptus*

*farrar straus giroux*
*new york*

# IMPROMPTUS

SELECTED

POEMS

AND

SOME

PROSE

## GOTTFRIED
## BENN

TRANSLATED

FROM THE

GERMAN

AND

EDITED

BY

MICHAEL

HOFMANN

Farrar, Straus and Giroux
18 West 18th Street, New York 10011

Gottfried Benn, *Sämtliche Werke*, copyright © 1986, 1987, 1989, 1991
Klett-Cotta – J. G. Cotta'sche Buchhandlung Nachfolger GmbH, Stuttgart
Gottfried Benn, *Statische Gedichte*, edited by Paul Raabe, copyright ©
1948, 2006 by Arche Literatur Verlag AG, Zurich/Hamburg
Translation, Introduction, and selection copyright © 2013 by Michael Hofmann
All rights reserved
Printed in the United States of America
First edition, 2013

Library of Congress Cataloging-in-Publication Data
Benn, Gottfried, 1886–1956.
    [Works. Selections. English]
    Impromptus : selected poems and some prose / Gottfried Benn ; translated
from the German and edited by Michael Hofmann. — First edition.
        pages  cm
    Includes index.
    ISBN 978-0-374-17537-5
    I. Hofmann, Michael, 1957 August 25– editor of compilation.  II. Title.

PT2603.E46 A2 2013
831'.912—dc23

                                                            2013021683

Designed by Quemadura

Farrar, Straus and Giroux books may be purchased for educational, business,
or promotional use. For information on bulk purchases, please contact the
Macmillan Corporate and Premium Sales Department at 1-800-221-7945,
extension 5442, or write to specialmarkets@macmillan.com.

www.fsgbooks.com
www.twitter.com/fsgbooks
www.facebook.com/fsgbooks

10 9 8 7 6 5 4 3 2 1

FOR CHRISTIAN WIMAN AND DON SHARE;

AND FOR ALAN JENKINS AND THE LATE MICK IMLAH

# CONTENTS

*prose*

# INTRODUCTION

THOUGH GOTTFRIED BENN can scarcely be said to exist in the English-speaking world, there are a surprising number of prominent mentions of him. T. S. Eliot, for instance, in his essay "The Three Voices of Poetry" goes so far as to associate one such voice—the first, "the voice of the poet talking to himself—or to nobody"—with Benn. John Berryman allows him the end of one Dream Song, no. 53: "and Gottfried Benn / said:—We are using our own skins for wallpaper and we cannot win." In his novel *Plexus* Henry Miller is careful to leave the 1927 issue of Eugene Jolas's avant-garde magazine, *transitions*, lying around, and quotes in extenso from Benn's essay in it. Frank O'Hara has a tilt at him in one of his invariably disastrous and perplexing diatribes, when he seems to have his ill-fitting Hector the Lecturer suit on: "Poetry is not instruments / that work at times / then walk out on you / laugh at you old / get drunk on you young / poetry's part of your self" ("To Gottfried Benn").

With all these appearances, you would have thought Benn had to have some being somewhere. But it's more like that space radiation called "chatter"; there's something that leads our instruments to think there's something "out there"; we might even give it a name, but most of us remain doubtful, and few of us expect ever to see it. I don't think you could fill a room with a conversation about Benn—non-Germans and non-Germanists, that is.

And yet we're talking of someone of the eminence of, say, Wallace Stevens, someone most Germans (and most German poets too) would concede as the greatest German poet since Rilke.

Basically, Benn has appeared once in English, namely in E. B. Ashton's edited collection of Benn's selected writings, *Primal Vision*, first published in 1958, and still in print with New Directions. The trouble with Ashton's book—and in this it perhaps betrays its origins in the postwar decade—is that it is not primarily interested in Benn the poet, but the man of ideas, the German, and the "phenotype." One has to wonder at the judgment and effectiveness (not to mention the long monopoly) of a book introducing a foreign poet to an English readership that is three parts prose, and where the translations of the poems (one-eighth of the whole) are starchy, cumbrous, and muted. They have neither the attack nor the ease of Benn in German—to me he is both the hardest and the softest poet who ever lived. Thus unsuccessfully transmitted, Benn has no English admirers; unlike Brecht, he's not even unpopular. It's only stray foreign readers like Joseph Brodsky or Adam Zagajewski, who read him in a third or fourth language, or in the original, who have anything like a true or a full sense of Benn.

Benn called his autobiography *Doppelleben*, but for once (see "Bauxite," see "Fragments 1955," see "Summa Summarum") he perhaps wasn't interested in counting, because I can see more like four of him: the military man, the doctor, the poet, and the ladies' man. With their different rhythms and urgencies and tolerances, these four identities—four suits of cards, two black, two red, two professional alibis, two passions, two kinds of truancy and two kinds of work—shaped and complicated his life. He ran from woman to woman, but also from woman to poem, from poem to uniform, from uniform to lab coat, and back again, and with all the possible variations. Style trumps facts, he said, and good stage management trumps fidelity. But within the constraints of his circumstances and especially his tightly drawn financial limits (very rarely in his life did he have money), he was at pains to be a gentleman (it's not a word one hears often nowadays, but it's a concept he certainly understood and tried to live by) and to lead an upright life: that is, one informed by distance and warmth and good presentation. Accordingly, the most important and longest-lasting relationship of his life was conducted largely by mail over twenty-four years with the Bremen businessman F. W. Oelze. Benn aspired—or resigned himself—to be at once an earl and a pariah. He was a brilliant and internationally acclaimed writer of poetry and prose who never came close to being able to live by it; a notably unenthusiastic doctor who nevertheless helped his "*Schmutzfinke von Patienten*" (his "squalid patients") as much as he could; an amorous and courtly man and an inveterate buyer of flowers for his wives and mistresses and casual liaisons; by his left eye he had the *Mensur*, the German dueling-scar, and twice—during the two world wars—he fell back into the army, where, ironically, he enjoyed the periods of greatest peace and productive contentment in his life.

Benn's first publication, in 1912—a small-press pamphlet called *Morgue and Other Poems*, one of the great debuts in literary history—catches him at a typical juncture: he had recently qualified as a medical doctor in Berlin; he was having an affair with the Jewish German poet and free spirit Else Lasker-Schüler;

and he was—if the reader will allow the expression, it's still more accurate than any other I can think of—moonlighting with the army, which had paid for his education. When World War I broke out, Benn, like so many others, quickly got hitched (though not to Lasker-Schüler), conceived a daughter (Nele was born in September 1915), and joined up again. For three years he was behind the lines in Brussels as a "doctor in a whorehouse." It was one of those immensely suggestive, paradigmatic times in his life when he was at once becalmed, isolated, and productive; the nation was distracted and engorged, but Benn was reading and writing. He writes about that period with grateful rapture, almost as though he were a medieval monk left to illuminate manuscripts behind stone walls a yard thick. After the war, he tried to find the same seclusion as a skin doctor and venereologist in private practice in Berlin, but that quality of *"béguinage"* (his word: a religious seclusion) remained something best provided by the army. Accordingly, in 1935, he tried the same thing again: left Berlin, re-enlisted, and, in 1938, remarried. In World War II, he fetched up at the fortress town of Landsberg an der Warthe (today the Polish town of Gorzów Wielkopolski), which he commemorated contemporaneously in the prose of "Block II, Room 66" ("Nothing so dreamy as barracks!"). There, underemployed by the army, as the senior medical man with the rank of colonel, while waiting for the German defeat he wrote poems, essays, and prose, among them many pieces that would certainly have cost him his liberty and most probably his life if they had been turned over to the SS.

A brief note on the vexed and controversial circumstances that restored him to the bosom of the army: Almost all his life, Benn had no expectations from governments (it's hard to imagine him voting, and impossible to guess which way); human existence was futile, progress a delusion, history a bloody mess, and the only stay against fatuity was art, was poetry. Writing should have no truck with any social or political aims. Anything less like the useful, obedient, and subsidized creature known as the "state poet" than Gottfried Benn is impossible to imagine. Then, in 1933 and 1934, Benn drifted into the Nazi orbit. For a brief while it looked to him as though his long-range ideas about the human species, his cultural pessimism, his Nietzschean and Spenglerian gloom, had somewhere to dock. He drafted a declaration of loyalty to the newly installed Nazi government that precipitated mass resignations from the Preußische Akademie der Künste, or Prussian Academy of Arts, to which he had only recently been elected; he addressed a sharp "reply to the literary émigrés" to (his adoring admirer) Klaus Mann; he gave a talk welcoming the Italian futurist (and Fascist) poet F. T. Marinetti to Berlin; he was briefly vice president of Hitler's Union Nationaler Schriftsteller, or Union of National Writers. Mutual disenchantment was not slow in coming; the relationship's fleeting appearance of compatibility shaded into, or gave way to, its natural level of implacable—and, for Benn, extremely threatening—mutual detestation. It dawned on Benn that the Nazis were not a bunch of pessimistic aesthetes like himself, but rather imbued with a sanguinary optimism; by the time of the Night of the Long Knives in June 1934, he was fully disabused. They, meanwhile, never forgave him for his early writings and his Jewish associations, got him struck off the medical register as a suspected Jew (Benn = Ben!), and banned him from writing altogether in 1938. They could hardly fail to find his work "degenerate," as they did that of his expressionist colleagues in the visual arts. At this point, Benn left Berlin and took refuge in the army, which in a typically stylish and abrasive phrase he described as "the aristocratic form of emigration." He wrote an analysis of suicides in the military. All this feels to me known, or partly known, understood or partly understood, in the English-speaking world. It remains an anomalous and troubling interval in his life, before, so to speak, normal disservice was resumed; to use it as grounds for not reading Benn—to play the "Fascist card"—is merely lazy and a little hysterical. Few of the modernists, after all, had the credentials of good democrats.

Most everything else in his life comes under the heading of "Herkunft, Lebenslauf—Unsinn!" ("background, CV—tosh!"), as he inimitably and contemptuously put it. Still, in the wake and a little in the manner of his contempt, here goes: father a clergyman, mother originally in service, from the French-speaking part of Switzerland. (In his dry, geneticist way, Benn makes as much of his mixed parentage as, say, Thomas Mann.) Born in one vicarage, grew up in another. The second of eight children, and the oldest son. Sent away to school at the age of ten. He studied religion at the behest of his father before being allowed to switch to literature and medicine. In 1914, he was a ship's doctor on a transatlantic steamship; he liked to claim he was so hard up he couldn't even afford to get off and tour New York. He was the doctor who, in 1916, officiated at the execution by a German firing squad of the British nurse Edith Cavell and her Belgian associate, who had been found guilty of treason for having helped Allied soldiers escape from German-occupied Belgium. The year 1922 saw the death of his mother from untreated breast cancer (see "Jena") and of his first wife, Edith Osterloh, from a botched appendectomy; the fact that he and Edith had lived separate lives didn't keep Benn from being deeply affected by her death. Incompetent or at least unambitious in most practical matters, he arranged to have their daughter Nele adopted by a Danish couple; toward the end of his life, he painstakingly rebuilt a relationship with her. In 1938, he married his second wife, Herta von Wedemeyer. Amid the confusion of the ending war, in July 1945, having been sent by Benn to the West for her own safety, Herta committed suicide, convinced she would fall into the hands of the Russians. Surely the poem "Death of Orpheus" owes something to her harrowing circumstances, and to Benn's grief and guilt. Following the defeat, occupation, and then partition of Germany, Benn returned to West Berlin, opened another medical practice, and married a third time: Ilse Kaul, a dentist. Because of his sometime pro-Nazi positions, he was not allowed to publish by the Allies: "undesirable then," he wrote, a little smugly, "undesirable again now." The Swiss publisher Arche brought out *Static Poems* in 1948, ushering in a great wave of Benn's late work. He was awarded the prestigious Georg Büchner Prize in 1951. In May 1956, his seventieth birthday was celebrated with the publication of a *Collected Poems*, beginning with the recently composed "Can Be No Sorrow." On July 7, 1956, at a time when the earth would indeed "yield easily to the spade," Gottfried Benn died in Berlin.

Benn's name is indissolubly connected to the German, or perhaps Nordic, movement of expressionism, like its direct contemporaries imagism and Dadaism a protomodern movement, but fiercer than the one and less theatrical than the other. Literary expressionism has almost as many meanings as it has practitioners, but in a general way (and certainly in Benn) it can be seen as a simultaneous boosting of both style and content. Expressionism is gaudy, neoprimitive, volatile, provocative, antirational. The brain is eclipsed by its older neighbors: the glands, the senses (including the oldest sense, the sense of smell). Expressionism is momentary, it doesn't count days or verify destinations. It might be the humdrum Baltic—shallowest and newest and saltiest of seas, sea beach to Berlin—but it feels like the Aegean, if not the South Pacific, in the poet's rhapsodic imagination. Expressionism hymns a simpler physis, the body under its own management. Down with the boardroom, away with the little pin-striped simpleton or puritan upstairs! Expressionism is an as-if, or an if-only: if only the body could write or paint or think! Or not think. Poems like "Express Train" or "Caryatid" or "Asters" are literary equivalents to the brash, paradisiac canvases of Emil Nolde or Ernst Ludwig Kirchner or Ferdinand Hodler.

Benn's very first poems were offcuts of *materia medica*: *Morgue* and *Fleisch* were among his titles, a prose book was called *Gehirne* (brains). As with a lot of expressionist writing, it was hard to see how it might develop, not least because it was already so fully and shockingly *there*: brash, confrontational, destructive, appalling. Benn wasn't sure either. In a splendidly saturnine note in his first collected works (the *Gesammelte Schriften* of 1922— he was thirty-five), he wrote: "Now these complete works, one volume, two hundred pages, thin stuff, one would be ashamed if one were still alive. No document worthy the name; I would be astonished if anyone were to read them; to me they are already very distant, I toss them behind me like Deucalion his stones; maybe human beings will emerge from the gargoyles; but whether they do or not, I shan't love them." I don't know that I have ever seen anything less self-enamored from a poet on his or her own work! In the event, something of what he so indifferently predicted did come to pass: "human beings" did emerge from the "gargoyles"—whether or not Benn loved them hardly matters. His later poems lost their ferocity, their shock, and their prankish, metallic manipulativeness; became softer, lived-in, improvised, gestured at, shuffling or shambling. They still had the same principal two ingredients: corpses (or mortality) and flowers; the same groping at one notion or another of a "beautiful youth." The "lavender aster" returns in the form of new flower complexes, as "drooping lilac . . . narcissus color, and smelling strongly of death," as poppies, phlox, gladioli, the "old and reliable ranunculi of Ostade," hydrangeas, and finally as forsythias and lilacs again, this time "with hope of roses." The beautiful or unbeautiful, loved or unloved cadavers have turned into Benn himself, anxiously remembering the ghosts of his salad days; or hoping to hold on, into June (of the year of his death—he died on July 7); or, in one of his last poems (the first one here, "Can Be No Sorrow"), thinking soberly and unflinchingly about the deaths of poets, put together from wood and tears and pain and spasm, the "sleep well" at once a close echo and a world away from the cynical "Rest easy" of "Little Aster."

During the 1920s and '30s, Benn found a way of parlaying his short, explosive free verse poems into lengthier, internal combustion pieces. His characteristic form became the tightly rhymed octave, often in very short two- or three-foot lines. The longings and strictures and surfeits articulated in these are often very beautiful and bizarre, but barely translatable, not even when there are equivalents—perhaps especially not when there are equivalents. Or what is the English, pray, for: "Banane, yes, Banane / vie méditerranée?" "Banana, yes, banana / Mediterranean life?" I don't think so. It is as though, having been done in one language (German?), it can never be done again, in any other! A blizzard of neologisms, incantatory and highly personal charm words, flower names, and technical terms; sociopathic hatred; a texture of fierce and luxurious depression. Benn pines for "Mediterranean," "Palau," "Night," "Cocaine," "Anesthesia." Life is "niederer Wahn," lower or lesser madness; in its place Benn calls for "thalassale Regression," for form, trance, elevation. It might seem Decadent, 1890s-style, only there is no pose about it, nothing effete. For all the Verlaine-like sonorities of the poems, there are ferocious energies at work within them. I am conscious that the poems of this period are underrepresented here. I'm afraid they were too difficult and idiosyncratic for me to carry them into English in any important way. I preferred to go, more or less directly, from the shocking early to the weary late: to those beerily misanthropic and magically beautiful mutterings of Benn's last two decades that have always particularly entranced me as a reader. Two world wars, two marriages, two bereavements, careers in the military and medicine, and forty years of writing have gone into their making. "Ausdruck und Stoffvernichtung," "expressiveness and destruction of subject matter" they are. They come with their own silence and space. Like the early poems, they are as they are, are as they want to be. The opposite of art, Benn always argued, is not actually nature but a concern to please.

Thus, the hardness of the early style—the "gargoyles"—is replaced by human tenderness, empathy, puzzlement, a kind of unfocused but unavoidable sadness. It is as though the poems themselves (and this strikes me as extremely rare in poetry, Eugenio Montale's late, *retrobottega* poems being a further instance) *are old*; have undergone an aging process, cellular and organic, like flesh. These later poems' resources—a mild, stoical plaintiveness, a burbling, flaccid syntax, an unsolicited melancholy, a heaping of negatives—are those of age; breathing and humming and carpet slippers and Juno cigarettes and murmuring and pain and a human smell have gone into them—not mere dime-a-dozen words. At bottom, life is unchanged in thousands of years: still solitude, still doubt, still want of recognition; poetry is always questioning and at odds with life; always "the insufferable / difficulties of outward-directed expression." You see the jowly man in front of his chaotic shelves. That "fascination" that Benn identified as the elusive but irreducible quality of poetry inheres in them as much as it does in the rhyming strophes; effectively, both are collages of the most varied and spirited diction. The growly misanthropic cuss who speaks them is as much an invention and a function of style as the brittle and glitteringly impersonal manner of the octaves. Although light as lace, they are wonderfully heavy with experience, "a pile of life in variegated forms."

Yeats says the poet "is never the bundle of accident and incoherence that sits down to breakfast; he has been reborn as an idea, something intended, complete." Really not so Benn, not in these last poems. He is absolutely the bundle seated—if not to breakfast exactly, then at least in the corner of the bar after work in the evening, where he downs two or three beers, smokes his Junos, listens to the radio, listens to the chatter of the other customers, scribbles something trenchantly doleful on a pad. It is rare for art to be so perspicuous, to be made from so extravagantly little—sometimes just "a dish / of sausage soup (free on Thursdays / with a beverage)"—so to pair grace with dailiness, discretion with intimacy, a shy wistfulness with stoicism.

Somehow, quite without my realizing it, I have spent half my life with Benn; back in his centenary year, 1986, I reviewed the two-volume edition of his poems and Holthusen's begun biography of him. He has influenced me, not only to translate him in the first place, but also while translating him. Over the years, thanks in part to Benn, my own sentences have become more indeterminate, my language more musical, my diction more florid. There is a sort of murmurous, *mi-voix*, *halblaut* quality in poems that I adore, and, languidly, strive for. I was all the time quietly being readied for a task I hardly dared suppose I would ever take on. I loved these poems when I first read and wrote about them half a lifetime ago; somehow—youth? trepidation? selfish possession rather than working to make them available to an English readership?—I never allowed myself to think I might actually translate them.

**MICHAEL HOFMANN**

*poems*

## KANN KEINE TRAUER SEIN

In jenem kleinen Bett, fast Kinderbett, starb die Droste
(zu sehn in ihrem Museum in Meersburg),
auf diesem Sofa Hölderlin im Turm bei einem Schreiner,
Rilke, George wohl in Schweizer Hospitalbetten,
in Weimar lagen die großen schwarzen Augen
Nietzsches auf einem weißen Kissen
bis zum letzten Blick –
alles Gerümpel jetzt oder garnicht mehr vorhanden,
unbestimmbar, wesenlos
im schmerzlos-ewigen Zerfall.

Wir tragen in uns Keime aller Götter,
das Gen des Todes und das Gen der Lust –
wer trennte sie: die Worte und die Dinge,
wer mischte sie: die Qualen und die Statt,
auf der sie enden, Holz mit Tränenbächen,
für kurze Stunden ein erbärmlich Heim.

Kann keine Trauer sein. Zu fern, zu weit,
zu unberührbar Bett und Tränen,
kein Nein, kein Ja,

## CAN BE NO SORROW

That narrow cot, hardly any bigger than a child's, is where
    Droste-Hülshoff died
(it's there in her museum in Meersburg),
on that sofa Hölderlin in his tower room at the carpenter's,
Rilke and George in hospital beds presumably, in Switzerland,
in Weimar, Nietzsche's great black eyes
rested on white pillows
till they looked their last—
all of it junk now, or no longer extant,
unattributable, anonymous
in its insentient and continual disintegration.

We bear within us the seeds of all the gods,
the gene of death and the gene of love—
who separated them, the words and the things,
who blended them, the torments and the place where they
    come to an end,
the few laths and the floods of tears,
home for a few wretched hours.

Can be no sorrow. Too distant, too remote,
bed and tears too impalpable,
no No, no Yes,

Geburt und Körperschmerz und Glauben
ein Wallen, namenlos, ein Huschen,
ein Überirdisches, im Schlaf sich regend,
bewegte Bett und Tränen —
schlafe ein!

birth and bodily pain and faith
an undefinable surge, a lurch,
an unearthly stirring in sleep
moved bed and tears—
sleep well!

JANUARY 6, 1956

1912-1920

## KLEINE ASTER

Ein ersoffener Bierfahrer wurde auf den Tisch gestemmt.
Irgendeiner hatte ihm eine dunkelhellila Aster
zwischen die Zähne geklemmt.
Als ich von der Brust aus
unter der Haut
mit einem langen Messer
Zunge und Gaumen herausschnitt,
muß ich sie angestoßen haben, denn sie glitt
in das nebenliegende Gehirn.
Ich packte sie ihm in die Brusthöhle
zwischen die Holzwolle,
als man zunähte.
Trinke dich satt in deiner Vase!
Ruhe sanft,
kleine Aster!

## LITTLE ASTER

A drowned drayman was hoisted onto the slab.
Someone had jammed a lavender aster
between his teeth.
As I made the incision up from the chest
with the long blade
under the skin
to cut out tongue and palate,
I must have nudged it because it slipped
into the brain lying adjacent.
I packed it into the thoracic cavity
with the excelsior
when he was sewn up.
Drink your fill in your vase!
Rest easy,
little aster!

## SCHÖNE JUGEND

Der Mund eines Mädchens, das lange im Schilf gelegen hatte,
sah so angeknabbert aus.
Als man die Brust aufbrach, war die Speiseröhre so löcherig.
Schließlich in einer Laube unter dem Zwerchfell
fand man ein Nest von jungen Ratten.
Ein kleines Schwesterchen lag tot.
Die andern lebten von Leber und Niere,
tranken das kalte Blut und hatten
hier eine schöne Jugend verlebt.
Und schön und schnell kam auch ihr Tod:
Man warf sie allesamt ins Wasser.
Ach, wie die kleinen Schnauzen quietschten!

## BEAUTIFUL YOUTH

The mouth of the girl who had lain long in the rushes
looked so nibbled.
When they opened her chest, her esophagus was so holey.
Finally in a bower under the diaphragm
they found a nest of young rats.
One little thing lay dead.
The others were living off kidneys and liver
drinking the cold blood and had
had themselves a beautiful youth.
And just as beautiful was their death, and quick:
the lot of them were thrown into the water.
Ah, will you hearken at the little muzzles' oinks!

# KREISLAUF

Der einsame Backzahn einer Dirne,
die unbekannt verstorben war,
trug eine Goldplombe.
Die übrigen waren wie auf stille Verabredung
ausgegangen.
Den schlug der Leichendiener sich heraus,
versetzte ihn und ging für tanzen.
Denn, sagte er,
nur Erde solle zur Erde werden.

## CIRCULATION

The solitary molar of a streetwalker
whose body had gone unclaimed
had a gold filling.
All the rest were gone,
as if by tacit agreement.
This one the morgue attendant snaffled for himself,
flogged it, and had himself a night out on the proceeds.
Because, so he said,
only clay should revert to clay.

# NACHTCAFÉ

824: Der Frauen Liebe und Leben.
Das Cello trinkt rasch mal. Die Flöte
rülpst tief drei Takte lang: das schöne Abendbrot.
Die Trommel liest den Kriminalroman zu Ende.

Grüne Zähne, Pickel im Gesicht
winkt einer Lidrandentzündung.

Fett im Haar
spricht zu offenem Mund mit Rachenmandel
Glaube Liebe Hoffnung um den Hals.

Junger Kropf ist Sattelnase gut.
Er bezahlt für sie drei Biere.

Bartflechte kauft Nelken,
Doppelkinn zu erweichen.

B-moll: die 35. Sonate.
Zwei Augen brüllen auf:
Spritzt nicht das Blut von Chopin in den Saal,
damit das Pack drauf rumlatscht!
Schluß! He, Gigi! —

# NIGHT CAFÉ

824: Lives and Loves of Women.
The cello takes a quick drink. The flute
Belches expansively for three beats: good old dinner.
The timpani has one eye on his thriller.

Mossed teeth in pimple face
Waves to incipient stye.

Greasy hair
Talks to open mouth with adenoids
Faith Love Hope round her neck.

Young goitre has a crush on saddlenose.
He treats her to onetwothree beers.

Sycosis brings carnations
To melt the heart of double chin.

B-flat minor: the 35th Sonata.
Two eyes yell:
Stop hosing the blood of Chopin round the room
For that rabble to slosh around in!
Enough! Hey, Gigi!—

Die Tür fließt hin: ein Weib.
Wüste ausgedörrt. Kanaanitisch braun.
Keusch. Höhlenreich. Ein Duft kommt mit. Kaum Duft.
Es ist nur eine süße Vorwölbung der Luft
gegen mein Gehirn.

Eine Fettleibigkeit trippelt hinterher.

The door melts away: a woman.
Dry desert. Canaanite tan.
Chaste. Concavities. A scent accompanies her, less a scent
Than a sweet pressure of the air
Against my brain.

An obesity waddles after.

## ALASKA

Europa, dieser Nasenpopel
aus einer Konfirmandennase,
wir wollen nach Alaska gehn.

Der Meermensch, der Urwaldmensch,
der alles aus seinem Bauch gebiert,
der Robben frißt, der Bären totschlägt,
der den Weibern manchmal was reinstößt:
der Mann.

## ALASKA

Europe, Europe's just a bogey in a confirmand's nose,
We're going to Alaska!

Ocean man, jungle man,
Gives birth to everything out of his belly,
Eats seal, shoots bear, from time to time
Shoves something up a woman:
A man.

## DER JUNGE HEBBEL

Ihr schnitzt und bildet: den gelenken Meißel
in einer feinen weichen Hand.
Ich schlage mit der Stirn am Marmorblock
die Form heraus,
meine Hände schaffen ums Brot.

Ich bin mir noch sehr fern.
Aber ich will Ich werden!
Ich trage einen tief im Blut,
der schreit nach seinen selbsterschaffenen
Götterhimmeln und Menschenerden.

Meine Mutter ist eine so arme Frau,
daß ihr lachen würdet, wenn ihr sie sähet,
wir wohnen in einer engen Bucht,
ausgebaut an des Dorfes Ende.
Meine Jugend ist mir wie ein Schorf:
eine Wunde darunter,
da sickert täglich Blut hervor.
Davon bin ich so entstellt.

Schlaf brauche ich keinen,
Essen nur so viel, daß ich nicht verrecke!

## THE YOUNG HEBBEL

You all carve and sculpt, the deft chisel
in a soft shapely hand.
I beat my head against the marble
to knock it into shape,
my hands work for a living.

I am still a long way from myself,
but I want to become Me!
There is someone deep in my blood
who cries out for homemade
Olympuses and worlds for humans.

My mother is such a poor wretch,
you'd laugh if you saw her,
we live in a tight annex,
built onto the end of the village.
My youth is like a scab:
under it there is a wound
that every day leaks blood.
It disfigures me.

I don't need sleep,
food just enough to keep from starving.

Unerbittlich ist der Kampf,
und die Welt starrt von Schwertspitzen.
Jede hungert nach meinem Herzen.
Jede muß ich, Waffenloser,
in meinem Blut zerschmelzen.

An implacable struggle
and the world bristling with sword points.
Each one hungers for my heart.
Each one, I, unarmed,
must melt in my blood.

## DROHUNG

Aber wisse:
Ich lebe Tiertage. Ich bin eine Wasserstunde.
Des Abends schläfert mein Lid wie Wald und Himmel.
Meine Liebe weiß nur wenig Worte:
Es ist so schön an deinem Blut.

## THREAT

Know this:
I live beast days. I am a water hour.
At night my eyelids droop like forest and sky.
My love knows few words:
I like it in your blood.

# GESÄNGE

## I

O daß wir unsere Ururahnen wären.
Ein Klümpchen Schleim in einem warmen Moor.
Leben und Tod, Befruchten und Gebären
glitte aus unseren stummen Säften vor.

Ein Algenblatt oder ein Dünenhügel,
vom Wind Geformtes und nach unten schwer.
Schon ein Libellenkopf, ein Möwenflügel
wäre zu weit und litte schon zu sehr.

## II

Verächtlich sind die Liebenden, die Spötter,
alles Verzweifeln, Sehnsucht, und wer hofft.
Wir sind so schmerzliche durchseuchte Götter
und dennoch denken wir des Gottes oft.

Die weiche Bucht. Die dunklen Wälderträume.
Die Sterne, schneeballblütengroß und schwer.
Die Panther springen lautlos durch die Bäume.
Alles ist Ufer. Ewig ruft das Meer –

## SONGS

I

O that we might be our ancestors' ancestors.
A clump of slime in a warm bog.
Life and death, fertilizing and giving birth
Would all be functions of our silent juices.

An algal leaf or a sand dune,
Shaped by the wind and basal and heavy-set.
Even a dragonfly's head or a gull's wing
Would be too evolved and suffer too much.

II

Contemptible are the lovers, the mockers,
All despair, yearning, and hope.
We are such painfully plague-ridden gods,
And yet we think continually of God.

The soft bay. The dark forest dreams.
The stars, snowball-blossom big and heavy.
Panthers lope silently among the trees.
Everything is strand. Forever calls the sea—

Da fiel uns Ikarus vor die Füße,
schrie: treibt Gattung, Kinder!
Rein ins schlechtgelüftete Thermopylä! –
Warf uns einen seiner Unterschenkel hinterher,
schlug um, war alle.

Then Icarus fell at our feet,
cried: Boys and girls, multiply!
Get into that poorly ventilated Thermopylae!—
He tossed one of his thighs at us,
flipped over, and was finished.

## D-ZUG

Braun wie Kognak. Braun wie Laub. Rotbraun. Malaiengelb.
D-Zug Berlin-Trelleborg und die Ostseebäder.

Fleisch, das nackt ging.
Bis in den Mund gebräunt vom Meer.
Reif gesenkt, zu griechischem Glück.
In Sichel-Sehnsucht: wie weit der Sommer ist!
Vorletzter Tag des neunten Monats schon!

Stoppel und letzte Mandel lechzt in uns.
Entfaltungen, das Blut, die Müdigkeiten,
die Georginennähe macht uns wirr.

Männerbraun stürzt sich auf Frauenbraun:

Ein Frau ist etwas für eine Nacht.
Und wenn es schön war, noch für die nächste!
Oh! Und dann wieder dies Bei-sich-selbst-sein!
Diese Stummheiten! Dies Getriebenwerden!

Eine Frau ist etwas mit Geruch.
Unsägliches! Stirb hin! Resede.
Darin ist Süden, Hirt und Meer.
An jedem Abhang lehnt ein Glück.

## EXPRESS TRAIN

Brown. Brandy-brown. Leaf-brown. Russet. Malayan yellow.
Express train Berlin–Trelleborg and the Baltic resorts.

Flesh that went naked.
Tanned unto the mouth by the sea.
Deeply ripened for Grecian joys.
How far along the summer, in sickle-submissiveness!
Penultimate day of the ninth month!

Athirst with stubble and last corn-shocks.
Unfurlings, blood, fatigue,
Deranged by dahlia-nearness.

Man-brown jumps on woman-brown.

A woman is something for a night.
And if you enjoyed it, then one more!
Oh! And then the return to one's own care.
The not-speaking! The urges!

A woman is something with a smell.
Ineffable! To die for! Mignonette.
Shepherd, sea, and South.
On every declivity a bliss.

Frauenhellbraun taumelt an Männerdunkelbraun:

Halte mich! Du, ich falle!
Ich bin im Nacken so müde.
Oh, dieser fiebernde süße
letzte Geruch aus den Gärten.

Woman-brown drapes itself on man-brown:

Hold me! I'm falling!
My neck is so weary.
Oh, the sweet last
Feverish scent from the gardens.

## ENGLISCHES CAFÉ

Das ganz schmalschuhige Raubpack,
Russinnen, Jüdinnen, tote Völker, ferne Küsten,
schleicht durch die Frühjahrsnacht.

Die Geigen grünen. Mai ist um die Harfe.
Die Palmen röten sich. Im Wüstenwind.

Rahel, die schmale Golduhr am Gelenk:
Geschlecht behütend und Gehirn bedrohend:
Feindin! Doch deine Hand ist eine Erde:
süßbraun, fast ewig, überweht vom Schoß.

Freundlicher Ohrring kommt. In Charme d'Orsay.
Die hellen Osterblumen sind so schön:
breitmäulig gelb, mit Wiese an den Füßen.

O Blond! O Sommer dieses Nackens! O
diese jasmindurchseuchte Ellenbeuge!
Oh, ich bin gut zu dir. Ich streichle
dir deine Schultern. Du, wir reisen:

Tyrrhenisches Meer. Ein frevelhaftes Blau.
Die Dorertempel. In Rosenschwangerschaft

## ENGLISCHES CAFÉ

The whole soft-shoe gaggle
Of Russians, Jewesses, dead peoples, distant coasts,
Slinks through the spring night.

The violins green. The harp plinks of May.
Palms blush in the desert simoom.

Rachel, slender wristwatch at the slender wrist,
Cupping her sex and menacing the brain.
Enemy. But your hand is earth:
Sweet brown, almost timeless, redolent of sex.

Kindly earring approaches. In Charme d'Orsay.
The daffodils are so beautiful.
A yellow gape, with meadows at their feet.

O blond! O the summer of that nape. O
Jessamine-drenched pulse points.
I am fond of you. I caress
Your shoulder. Let's go:

Tyrrhenian Sea. A conspirative blue.
Doric temples. The plains

die Ebenen. Felder
sterben den Asphodelentod.

Lippen, verschwärmt und tiefgefüllt wie Becher,
als zögerte das Blut des süßen Orts,
rauschen durch eines Mundes ersten Herbst.

O wehe Stirn! Du Kranke, tief im Flor
der dunklen Brauen! Lächle, werde hell:
die Geigen schimmern einen Regenbogen.

Pregnant with roses. Fields
Die asphodel deaths.

Lips abuzz and deeply filled as goblets,
As though the blood first hesitated at the sweet spot,
Then coursed through the first autumn of a mouth.

O weary head. Invalid, deep in the mourning
Of your swart brows. Smile, brighten, why don't you:
The violins are sawing a rainbow.

## KURKONZERT

Über Krüppel und Badeproleten,
Sonnenschirme, Schoßhunde, Boas,
über das Herbstmeer und das Grieg-Lied:
Ob Iris kommt?

Sie friert. Der kleine graue Stock in ihrer Hand
friert mit. Wird Klein. Will tiefer in die Hand.

Du, Glockenblumen in den Schal gebunden,
das weiße Kreuz aus Scheitel und aus Zähnen
liegt, wenn du lachst, so süß in deinem Braun!

Du steiles, weißes Land! O Marmorlicht!
Du rauschst so an mein Blut. Du helle Bucht!

Die große Müdigkeit der Schulterblätter!
Die Zärtlichkeit des Rockes um ihr Knie!
Du rosa Staub! Du Ufer mit Libellen!
Du, von den Flächen einer Schale steigend.
Im Veilchenschurz. Von Brüsten laut umblüht.

O Herbst und Heimkehr über diesem Meer!
Die Gärten sinken um. Machtloser grauer Strand.

## SPA CONCERT

Quite transcending the cripples and the spa proles,
The parasols, lapdogs, and feather boas,
The autumn sea and the wretched Grieg,
The question: Will Iris come?

She is cold. The little cane in her hand
Is cold. Shivers. Wants to shrink into her hand.

You, with bellflowers woven in your scarf,
The white cross of your parted hair and teeth
Contrasts so prettily with your tan when you laugh!

You white, cliffy land! Marmoreal light!
You make my blood drunk! Bright bay!

The great lassitude of the shoulder blades!
The tenderness of the skirts about her knees!
O pink dust! Dragonfly coast!
You, ascending steeply off the planes of a hollow.
In violet loincloth. Rowdily breast-crested.

O autumn and homecoming over the sea!
The gardens subside. Gray strand without power.

Kein Boot, kein Segel geht.
Wer nimmt mich winters auf?
Aus so viel Fernen zusammengeweht,
auf so viel Sternen neu geboren
bis vor dies Ufer: – Iris geht.

No boat, no sail abroad.
Who will take me in for the winter?
Blown together from so many distances,
Reconfigured on so many stars
Before this shore. Iris goes.

## KARYATIDE

Entrücke dich dem Stein! Zerbirst
die Höhle, die dich knechtet! Rausche
doch in die Flur! Verhöhne die Gesimse –
sieh: durch den Bart des trunkenen Silen
aus einem ewig überrauschten
lauten einmaligen durchdröhnten Blut
träuft Wein in seine Scham!

Bespei die Säulensucht: toderschlagene
greisige Hände bebten sie
verhangenen Himmeln zu. Stürze
die Tempel vor die Sehnsucht deines Knies,
in dem der Tanz begehrt!

Breite dich hin, zerblühe dich, oh, blute
dein weiches Beet aus großen Wunden hin:
sieh, Venus mit den Tauben gürtet
sich Rosen um der Hüften Liebestor –
sieh dieses Sommers letzten blauen Hauch
auf Astermeeren an die fernen
baumbraunen Ufer treiben; tagen
sieh diese letzte Glück-Lügenstunde
unserer Südlichkeit
hochgewölbt.

## CARYATID

Renege on the rock! Smash
The oppressor cave! Sashay
Out onto the floor! Scorn the cornices—
See, from the beard of drunk Silenus,
From the unique uproar of his blood,
The wine dribble onto his genitals!

Spit on the obsession with pillars:
Ancient rheumatic hands quake toward
Gray skies. Bring down the temple
By the yearning of your knees
Twitching with dance.

Spill, spread, unpetal, bleed
Your soft flowers through great wounds.
Venus with her doves girds her loins
With roses—
See the summer's last puff of blue
Drift on seas of asters to distant
Tree-brown coasts; see
This final hour of our deceitful
Southern happiness
Held aloft.

**1922–1936**

# JENA

„Jena vor uns im lieblichen Tale"
schrieb meine Mutter von einer Tour
auf einer Karte vom Ufer der Saale,
sie war in Kösen im Sommer zur Kur;
nun längst vergessen, erloschen die Ahne,
selbst ihre Handschrift, Graphologie,
Jahre des Werdens, Jahre der Wahne,
nur diese Worte vergesse ich nie.

Es war kein berühmtes Bild, keine Klasse,
für lieblich sah man wenig blühn,
schlechtes Papier, keine holzfreie Masse,
auch waren die Berge nicht rebengrün,
doch kam man vom Lande, von kleinen Hütten,
so waren die Täler wohl lieblich und schön,
man brauchte nicht Farbdruck, man brauchte nicht Bütten,
man glaubte, auch andere würden es sehn.

Es war wohl ein Wort von hoher Warte,
ein Ausruf hatte die Hand geführt,
sie bat den Kellner um eine Karte,
so hatte die Landschaft sie berührt,

## JENA

"Jena before us in the lovely valley"
Thus my mother on a postcard
From a walking holiday on the banks of the Saale,
She was spending a week at the spa of Kösen;
Long forgotten now, the ancestor no more,
Her script a subject for graphology,
Years of becoming, years of illusion,
Only those words I'll never forget.

It wasn't a great picture, no class,
There was not enough blossom
To justify lovely, poor paper, no pulp-free mass,
Also the hills weren't green with vineyards,
But she was from backcountry hovels,
So the valleys probably did strike her as lovely,
She didn't need laid paper or four-color print,
She supposed others would see what she had seen.

It was something said at a venture,
An exaltation had prompted it,
The landscape had moved her,
So she asked the waiter for a postcard,

und doch — wie oben — erlosch die Ahne
und das gilt allen und auch für den,
die — Jahre des Werdens, Jahre der Wahne —
heute die Stadt im Tale sehn.

And yet—*vide supra*—the ancestor went on,
As will we all, including even those—
Years of becoming, years of illusion—
Who see the town in the valley today.

## EINSAMER NIE –

Einsamer nie als im August:
Erfüllungsstunde – im Gelände
die roten und die goldenen Brände
doch wo ist deiner Gärten Lust?

Die Seen hell, die Himmel weich,
die Äcker rein und glänzen leise,
doch wo sind Sieg und Siegsbeweise
aus dem von dir vertretenen Reich?

Wo alles sich durch Glück beweist
und tauscht den Blick und tauscht die Ringe
im Weingeruch, im Rausch der Dinge –:
dienst du dem Gegenglück, dem Geist.

## NEVER LONELIER

Never lonelier than in August:
Hour of plenitude—the countryside
Waving with red and golden tassels,
But where is your pleasure garden?

Soft skies and sparkling lakes,
The healthy sheen of fields,
But where is the pomp and display
Of the empire you represent?

Everything lays claim to happiness,
Swaps glances, swaps rings
In wine-breath, in the intoxication of things;
You serve the counter-happiness, the intellect.

## ASTERN

Astern — schwälende Tage,
alte Beschwörung, Bann,
die Götter halten die Waage
eine zögernde Stunde an.

Noch einmal die goldenen Herden
der Himmel, das Licht, der Flor,
was brütet das alte Werden
unter den sterbenden Flügeln vor?

Noch einmal das Ersehnte,
den Rausch, der Rosen Du —
der Sommer stand und lehnte
und sah den Schwalben zu,

noch einmal ein Vermuten,
wo längst Gewißheit wacht:
die Schwalben streifen die Fluten
und trinken Fahrt und Nacht.

## ASTERS

Asters—sweltering days
Old adjuration / curse,
The gods hold the balance
For an uncertain hour.

Once more the golden flocks
Of heaven, the light, the trim—
What is that ancient process
Hatching under its dying wings?

Once more the yearned-for,
The intoxication, the rose of you,
Summer leaned in the doorway
Watching the swallows,

One more presentiment
Where certainty is not hard to come by:
Wing tips brush the face of the waters,
Swallows sip speed and night.

## TURIN

„Ich laufe auf zerrissenen Sohlen",
schrieb dieses große Weltgenie
in seinem letzten Brief – dann holen
sie ihn nach Jena – Psychiatrie.

Ich kann mir keine Bücher kaufen,
ich sitze in den Librairien:
Notizen – dann nach Aufschnitt laufen: –
das sind die Tage von Turin.

Indes Europas Edelfäule
an Pau, Bayreuth und Epsom sog,
umarmte er zwei Droschkengäule,
bis ihn sein Wirt nach Hause zog.

## TURIN

"I'm on my uppers,"
Wrote the world-class genius
In his last letter—then they haul
Him off to Jena—psychiatry calls.

I can't afford to buy books;
I sit around in public libraries,
Scribble notes, then go for cold cuts,
These are the days of Turin.

While Europe's noble rot
Supped at Pau, Bayreuth, and Epsom,
He put his arms round two cart-
Horses, until his landlord dragged him home.

**1937–1947**

## ACH, DAS FERNE LAND –

Ach, das ferne Land,
wo das Herzzerreißende
auf runden Kiesel
oder Schilffläche libellenflüchtig
anmurmelt,
auch der Mond
verschlagenen Lichts
– halb Reif, halb Ährenweiß –
den Doppelgrund der Nacht
so tröstlich anhebt –

ach, das ferne Land,
wo vom Schimmer der Seen
die Hügel warm sind,
zum Beispiel Asolo, wo die Duse ruht,
von Pittsburgh trug sie der „Duilio" heim,
alle Kriegsschiffe, auch die englischen, flaggten halbmast,
als er Gibraltar passierte –

dort Selbstgespräche
ohne Beziehungen auf Nahes,
Selbstgefühle,

## AH, THE FARAWAY LAND—


Ah, the faraway land,
where heartbreak
comes to rest
dragonfly-fleetingly
on round pebble
or murmurous reed-bed,
and the moon
with its oblique light
—half frost, half cream of wheat—
casts the background of night
into such soothing relief—

ah, the faraway land,
where the hills are warmed
by the shimmering reflection of the lakes,
as for instance Asolo, where la Duse slumbers—
when the *Duilio* carried her home from Pittsburgh,
all the warships, even the British, flagged at half-mast
as she passed through the Straits—

self-communing there
without taking in anything to hand,
sense of selfhood,

frühe Mechanismen,
Totemfragmente
in die weiche Luft

etwas Rosinenbrot im Rock —
so fallen die Tage,
bis der Ast am Himmel steht,
auf dem die Vögel einruhn
nach langem Flug.

early mechanisms,
totem fragments
in the soft air—

an end of raisin bread in your coat—
and so the days pass,
till there stands out against the sky the bough
on which the birds rest,
their long flight done.

## CHOPIN

Nicht sehr ergiebig im Gespräch,
Ansichten waren nicht seine Stärke,
Ansichten reden drum herum,
wenn Delacroix Theorien entwickelte,
wurde er unruhig, er seinerseits konnte
die Notturnos nicht begründen.

Schwacher Liebhaber;
Schatten in Nohant,
wo George Sands Kinder
keine erzieherischen Ratschläge
von ihm annahmen.

Brustkrank in jener Form
mit Blutungen und Narbenbildung,
die sich lange hinzieht;
stiller Tod
im Gegensatz zu einem
mit Schmerzparoxysmen
oder durch Gewehrsalven:
man rückte den Flügel (Erard) an die Tür
und Delphine Potocka
sang ihm in der letzten Stunde
ein Veilchenlied.

## CHOPIN

Not much of a conversationalist,
ideas weren't his strong suit,
ideas miss the point,
when Delacroix expounded his theories
it made him nervous, he for his part
could offer no explanation of the Nocturnes.

A poor lover;
mere shadow in Nohant
where George Sand's children
rejected his attempts
at discipline.

His tuberculosis
took the chronic form,
with repeated bleeding and scarring;
a creeping death,
as opposed to one
in convulsions of agony
or by firing squad:
the piano (Erard) was pushed back against the door
and Delphine Potocka
sang him
Mozart's *Veilchenlied* in his last hour.

Nach England reiste er mit drei Flügeln:
Pleyel, Erard, Broadwood,
spielte für 20 Guineen abends
eine Viertelstunde
bei Rothschilds, Wellingtons, im Strafford House
und vor zahllosen Hosenbändern;
verdunkelt von Müdigkeit und Todesnähe
kehrte er heim
auf den Square d'Orléans.

Dann verbrennt er seine Skizzen
und Manuskripte,
nur keine Restbestände, Fragmente, Notizen,
diese verräterischen Einblicke –
sagte zum Schluß:
„meine Versuche sind nach Maßgabe dessen vollendet,
was mir zu erreichen möglich war."

Spielen sollte jeder Finger
mit der seinem Bau entsprechenden Kraft,
der vierte ist der schwächste
(nur siamesisch zum Mittelfinger).
Wenn er begann, lagen sie
auf e, fis, gis, h, c.

Wer je bestimmte Präludien
von ihm hörte,
sei es in Landhäusern oder
in einem Höhengelände

He took three pianos with him to England:
Pleyel, Erard, Broadwood,
for twenty guineas
he would give fifteen-minute recitals in the evenings
at the Rothschilds' and the Wellingtons', in Strafford House
to the assembled cummerbunds;
then, dark with fatigue and imminent death,
he went home
to the Square d'Orleans.

There he burned his sketches
and manuscripts,
didn't want any leftover scraps
betraying him—
at the end he said:
"I have taken my experiment
as far as it was possible for me to go."

Each finger was to play
to no more than its natural strength,
the fourth being the weakest
(twinned with the middle finger).
At the start, they occupied the keys
of E, F-sharp, G-sharp, B, and C.

Anyone hearing
certain of his Preludes
in country seats or
at altitude,

oder aus offenen Terrassentüren
beispielsweise aus einem Sanatorium,
wird es schwer vergessen.

Nie eine Oper komponiert,
keine Symphonie,
nur diese tragischen Progressionen
aus artistischer Überzeugung
und mit einer kleinen Hand.

through open French windows
on the terrace, say, of a sanatorium,
will not easily forget it.

He composed no operas,
no symphonies,
only those tragic progressions
from artistic conviction
and with a small hand.

## ORPHEUS' TOD

Wie du mich zurückläßt, Liebste –
von Erebos gestoßen,
dem unwirtlichen Rhodope
Wald herziehend,
zweifarbige Beeren,
rotglühendes Obst –
Belaubung schaffend,
die Leier schlagend
den Daumen an der Saite!

Drei Jahre schon im Nordsturm!
An Totes zu denken, ist süß,
so Entfernte,
man hört die Stimme reiner,
fühlt die Küsse,
die flüchtigen und die tiefen –
doch du irrend bei den Schatten!

Wie du mich zurückläßt –
anstürmen die Flußnymphen,
anwinken die Felsenschönen,
gurren: „im öden Wald
nur Faune und Schratte, doch du,

## DEATH OF ORPHEUS

How can you leave me, darling—
sent packing by the nether slopes of Erebus
to drift around the inhospitable forests
of Rhodope,
parti-colored berries,
red-glowing fruit—
gathering foliage,
striking the lyre,
my thumb on the strings!

Three years in the biting north wind!
To think of the dead is sweet,
my so-removed one,
I hear your voice more clearly,
feel your kisses,
both the fleeting and the thorough—
but the thought of you among the shades!

How can you leave me—
to the naiads' onslaught,
the blandishments of the cliff-face beauties,
their cooing: "in the bleak woods
only fauns and wood-sprites, but you,

Sänger, Aufwölber
von Bronzelicht, Schwalbenhimmeln –
fort die Töne –
Vergessen –!"


– drohen –!


Und eine starrt so seltsam.
Und eine Große, Gefleckte,
bunthäutig („gelber Mohn")
lockt unter Demut, Keuschheitsandeutungen
bei hemmungsloser Lust – (Purpur
im Kelch der Liebe –!) vergeblich!


drohen –!


Nein, du sollst nicht verrinnen,
du sollst nicht übergehn in
Iole, Dryope, Prokne,
die Züge nicht vermischen mit Atalanta,
daß ich womöglich Eurydike
stammle bei Lais –


doch: drohen –!


und nun die Steine
nicht mehr der Stimme folgend,
dem Sänger,
mit Moos sich hüllend,

singer of bronze light,
constellator of swallow-teeming skies—
put away your song—
forget!"

—threaten—!

One sends me such meaning looks.
And another, well-built, freckled,
probably mixed-race ("it's called yellow poppy"),
beckons demurely, suggests chaste games
and means rampant desire—("inspect my love chalice's
purple!"—forget it, baby!)

—they threaten—!

No, you're not to be diluted,
you're not to blur
into Iole, Dryope, Procne,
nor mix your features with Atalanta's,
I don't want to blurt out your name inappropriately
when I'm with some Lais—

but: they threaten me—!

and now the stones
no more obedient to my voice,
the singer's,
no more swaddling themselves in moss,

die Äste laubbeschwichtigt,
die Hacken ährenbesänftigt —:
nackte Haune —!

nun wehrlos dem Wurf der Hündinnen,
der wüsten —
nun schon die Wimper naß,
der Gaumen blutet —
und nun die Leier —
hinab den Fluß —

die Ufer tönen —

cudgels not soothed with leafage,
no scythes muffled with ears of corn—:
naked flails—!

helpless now against the whelps of bitches,
the merciless—
lashes wet,
gums bloodied—
and now the lyre—
downstream—

the echoing banks—

# SEPTEMBER

I

Du, über den Zaun gebeugt mit Phlox
(vom Regenguß zerspalten,
seltsamen Wildgeruchs),
der gern auf Stoppeln geht,
zu alten Leuten tritt,
die Balsaminen pflücken,
Rauch auf Feldern
mit Lust und Trauer atmet –

aufsteigenden Gemäuers,
das noch sein Dach vor Schnee und Winter will,
kalklöschenden Gesellen
ein: „ach, vergebens" zuzurufen
nur zögernd sich verhält –

gedrungen eher als hochgebaut,
auch unflätigen Kürbis nackt am Schuh,
fett und gesichtslos, dies Krötengewächs –

Ebenen-entstiegener,
Endmond aller Flammen,

## SEPTEMBER

I

You, leaning over the fence and the phlox
(split by the rain,
smelling strangely feral),
given to walking on stubble fields,
going up to old people
plucking balsamines,
inhaling smoke on plowland
with pleasure and sorrow—

walls going up
meaning to be roofed before the onset of snow and winter,
apprentices slaking lime,
calling out to them: "Why bother,"
then shyly stifling it—

not lofty, squat,
and a shapeless pumpkin by your foot,
fat and featureless, blebbed growth—

escapee from the plains,
terminal moon of flame,

aus Frucht- und Fieberschwellungen
abfallend, schon verdunkelten Gesichts –
Narr oder Täufer,
des Sommers Narr, Nachplapperer, Nachruf
oder der Gletscher Vorlied,
jedenfalls Nußknacker,
Schilfmäher,
Beschäftigter mit Binsenwahrheiten –

vor dir der Schnee,
Hochschweigen, unfruchtbar
die Unbesambarkeit der Weite:
da langt dein Arm hin,
doch über den Zaun gebeugt
die Kraut- und Käferdränge,
das Lebenwollende,
Spinnen und Feldmäuse –


II


Du, ebereschenverhangen
von Frühherbst,
Stoppelgespinst,
Kohlweißlinge im Atem,
laß viele Zeiger laufen,
Kuckucksuhren schlagen,
lärme mit Vespergeläut,
gonge

shriveling from fruit- and fever-swellings,
already dark-complexioned—
fool or baptist,
summer's fool, babbler, obit
or hymn to glaciers,
in any case nutcracker,
reed-mower,
purveyor of self-evident truths—

before you the snow,
profound silence,
unfruitful expanses.
You reach out for it,
but leaning over the fence,
seethe of weed and beetle,
the lust for life
of spiders and field mice—


II


You, mountain-ash hung
from Indian summer,
stubbly ghost,
cabbage whites in your breath,
let many hands tick,
cuckoo clocks strike,
bells din for evensong,
gong

die Stunde, die so golden feststeht,
so bestimmt dahinbräunt,
in ein zitternd Herz!

Du: – Anderes!
So ruhn nur Götter
oder Gewänder
unstürzbarer Titanen
langgeschaffener,
so tief eingestickt
Falter und Blumen
in die Bahnen!

Oder ein Schlummer früher Art,
als kein Erwachen war,
nur goldene Wärme und Purpurbeeren,
benagt von Schwalben, ewigen,
die nie von dannen ziehn –
Dies schlage, gonge,
diese Stunde,
denn
wenn du schweigst,
drängen die Säume herab
pappelbestanden und schon kühler.

the hour so fixed and golden,
so definitively weathered,
to a trembling heart!

You—other!
Only gods
or tunics
of invincible Titans
rest so,
long-made,
so deeply sewn into
the tracks of flowers and moths!

Or slumber of an earlier kind,
when there was no awakening,
only golden warmth and purple berries
nibbled by perennial swallows
that never migrate—
Sound it, gong it,
this hour,
because when you cease,
the edges of the fields will encroach,
poplar-grown and chill.

## NACHZEICHNUNG

I

O jene Jahre! Der Morgen grünes Licht,
auch die noch nicht gefegten Lusttrottoire –
der Sommer schrie von Ebenen in der Stadt
und sog an einem Horn,
das sich von oben füllte.

Lautlose Stunde. Wässrige Farben
eines hellgrünen Aug's verdünnten Strahls,
Bilder aus diesem Zaubergrün, gläserne Reigen:
Hirten und Weiher, eine Kuppel, Tauben –
gewoben und gesandt, erglänzt, erklungen –,
verwandelbare Wolken eines Glücks!

So standest du vor Tag: die Spring-
brunnen noch ohne Perlen, tatenlos
Gebautes und die Steige; die Häuser
verschlossen, du *erschufst*
den Morgen, jasminene Frühe,
sein Jauchzen, uranfänglich
sein Strahl – noch ohne Ende – o jene Jahre!

# TRACING

I

O those years! The green light of morning
and the still-unswept pavements—
summer yelled from every surface of the city
and supped at a horn
refilled from above.

Silent hour. Watery colors
of a pale green eye's diluted stream,
scenes picked out in that magic green, glass dances,
shepherds and ponds, pigeons, a cupola—
woven, dispatched, shining, faded—
mutable clouds of happiness!

So you faced the day: the font
without bubbles, the frontages
loom without you; the houses
locked, it was for you to create
the morning, early jasmine,
its yelps, its incipient aboriginal
stream—still without end—O the years!

Ein Unauslöschliches im Herzen,
Ergänzungen vom Himmel und der Erde;
Zuströmendes aus Schilf und Gärten,
Gewitter abends
tränkten die Dolden ehern,
die barsten dunkel, gespannt von ihren Seimen;
und Meer und Strände,
bewimpelte mit Zelten,
glühenden Sandes trächtig,
bräunende Wochen, gerbend alles
zu Fell für Küsse, die niedergingen
achtlos und schnell verflogen
wie Wolkenbrüche!

Darüber hing die Schwere
auch jetzt — doch Trauben
aus ihr,

die Zweige niederziehend und wieder hochlassend,
nur einige Beeren,
wenn du mochtest,
erst —

noch nicht so drängend und überhangen
von kolbengroßen Fruchtfladen,
altem schwerem Traubenfleisch —

o jene Jahre!

Something unquenchable in the heart,
playing to you from reeds and gardens,
complement to heaven and earth;
evening storms
drenched the brassy umbels,
darkly they burst, taut with seeds,
and sea and strands,
wimpled with tents,
full of burning sand,
weeks bronzing, tanning everything
to pelts for kisses landing
indiscriminately like cloudbursts
and soon over!

Above hung a weight
even then grapes
dangling,

pulling down the tendrils and letting them rebound,
only a few berries
if you wanted,
at first—

not yet so bulging and overhung with
plate-sized bunches,
old heavy grape-flesh—

O the years!

Dunkle Tage des Frühlings,
nicht weichender Dämmer um Laub;
Fliederblüte gebeugt, kaum hochblickend
narzissenfarben und starken Todesgeruchs,
Glückausfälle,
sieglose Trauer des Unerfüllten.

Und in den Regen hinein,
der auf das Laub fällt,
höre ich ein altes Wälderlied,
von Wäldern, die ich einst durchfuhr
und wiedersah, doch ich ging nicht
in die Halle, wo das Lied erklungen war,
die Tasten schwiegen längst,
die Hände ruhten irgendwo,
gelöst von jenen Armen, die mich hielten,
zu Tränen rührten,
Hände aus den Oststeppen,
blutig zertretenen längst –
nur noch ihr Wälderlied
in den Regen hinein
an dunklen Tagen des Frühlings
den ewigen Steppen zu.

II

Dark days of spring,
impenetrable murk in the leaves;
drooping lilac, barely looking up
narcissus color, and smelling strongly of death,
loss of content,
untriumphant sadness of the unfulfilled.

And in the rain
falling on the leaves
I hear an old song—
of forests once crossed
and revisited, but not
the hall where they were singing,
the keys were silent,
the hands were resting somewhere
apart from the arms that held me,
moved me to tears,
hands from the eastern steppes,
long since trampled and bloody—
only their singing
in the rain,
dark days of spring,
everlasting steppes.

## ST. PETERSBURG –
## MITTE DES JAHRHUNDERTS

„Jeder, der einem anderen hilft,
ist Gethsemane,
jeder, der einen anderen tröstet,
ist Christi Mund",
singt die Kathedrale des heiligen Isaak,
das Alexander-Newsky-Kloster,
die Kirche des heiligen Peter und Paul,
in der die Kaiser ruhn,
sowie die übrigen hundertzweiundneunzig griechischen,
acht römisch-katholischen,
eine anglikanische, drei armenische,
lettische, schwedische, estnische,
finnische Kapellen.

Wasserweihe
der durchsichtigen blauen Newa
am Dreikönigstag.
Sehr gesundes Wasser, führt die fremden Stoffe ab.
Trägt die herrlichen Schätze heran
für das Perlmutterzimmer,
das Bernsteinzimmer
von Zarskoje Selo

## ST. PETERSBURG —
## MID-CENTURY

"Each of you who helps another
is Gethsemane,
each of you who comforts another
is the mouth of Christ,"
they sing in St. Isaac's Cathedral,
the Alexander Nevsky Monastery,
the church of Peter and Paul
where the emperors rest,
and in the remaining one hundred and twenty-nine Orthodox,
eight Roman Catholic,
one Anglican, three Armenian,
Lithuanian, Swedish, Estonian,
and Finnish chapels.

Blessing
of the clear blue Neva
on the day of Three Kings.
The water is very healthy, it washes away all impurities.
Ferries the wonderful treasures
for the Mother-of-Pearl Room,
the Amber Room
in Tsarskoye Selo

in den Duderhoffschen Bergen,
den himmelblauen sibirischen Marmor
für die Freitreppen.
Kanonensalven
wenn sie auftaut,
Tochter der Seen
Onega und Ladoga!

Vormittagskonzert im Engelhardtschen Saal,
Madame Stepanow,
die Glinkas „Das Leben für den Zaren"
kreiert hatte, schreit unnatürlich,
Worojews Bariton hat schon gelitten.
An einem Pfeiler,
mit vorstehenden weißen Zähnen,
afrikanischer Lippe,
ohne Brauen,
Alexander Sergeitsch (Puschkin).

Neben ihm Baron Brambeus,
dessen „großer Empfang beim Satan"
als Gipfel der Vollkommenheit gilt.
Violoncellist: Davidoff.
Und dann die russischen Bässe: ultratief,
die normalen Singbässe vielfach in der Oktave
verdoppelnd,
das Contra-C rein und voll,
aus zwanzig Kehlen
ultratief.

in the Duderhoff Hills,
the sky-blue Siberian marble
for the steps.
Twenty-one-gun salutes
when the ice melts,
the daughter of Lakes
Onega and Ladoga!

Morning concert in the Engelhardt Room,
Mme. Stepanov,
who has created Glinka's *Life for the Tsar*
screams unnaturally,
Voroyev's baritone has suffered.
Leaning against a pillar,
with protuberant white teeth,
thick African lips,
no eyebrows,
stands Alexander Sergeyevich (Pushkin).

Beside him Baron Brambeus
whose "great reception at Satan's"
is counted the height of perfection.
Cellist: Davidoff.
And then the Russian basses: extra low,
often a full octave below the standard basses,
the counter-C pure and clear
from twenty throats,
extra low.

Zu den Inseln!

Namentlich Krestowsky – Lustort, Lustwort –,

Baschkiren, Bartrussen, Rentiersamojeden

auf Sinnlichkeits- und Übersinnlichkeitserwerb!

Erster Teil:

„Vom Gorilla bis zur Vernichtung Gottes",

zweiter Teil:

„Von der Vernichtung Gottes bis zur Verwandlung

des physischen Menschen" –

Kornschnaps!

Das Ende der Dinge

ein Branntweinschluckauf

ultratief!


Raskolnikow

(als Ganzes weltanschaulich stark bedrängt)

betritt Kabak,

ordinäre Kneipe.

Klebrige Tische,

Ziehharmonika,

Dauertrinker,

Säcke unter den Augen,

einer bittet ihn

„zu einer vernünftigen Unterhaltung",

Heuabfälle im Haar.

(Anderer Mörder:

Dorian Gray, London,

Geruch des Flieders,

honigfarbener Goldregen

To the islands!
Krestovsky—cesspool of vice!—
Bashkirs, bearded Russians, reindeer Samoyed
for purposes of sensuality and hypersensuality!
First part:
"From the gorilla to the destruction of God,"
second part:
"From the destruction of God to the transformation
of physical man"
corn brandy!
The end of things
hiccuping brandy
extra low!

Raskolnikov
(ontologically under strain)
sets foot in Kabak,
a low bar.
Sticky tables,
harmonica,
all-day drinkers,
bags under their eyes,
one of them invites him
"to a sensible conversation,"
hayseeds in his hair.
(Another murderer:
Dorian Gray, Esq., London,
smell of lilac,
honey-colored laburnum

am Haus – Parktraum –
betrachtet Ceylonrubin für Lady B.,
bestellt Gamelanorchester.)

Raskolnikow,
stark versteift,
wird erweckt durch Sonja „mit dem gelben Billett"
(Prostituierte. Ihr Vater
steht der Sache „im Gegenteil tolerant gegenüber"),
sie sagt:
„Steh auf! Komm sofort mit!
Bleib am Kreuzweg stehn,
küsse die Erde, die du besudelt,
vor der du gesündigt hast,
verneige dich dann vor aller Welt,
sage allen laut:
ich bin der Mörder –
willst du?
Kommst du mit?" –
und er kam mit.

Jeder, der einen anderen tröstet,
ist Christi Mund –

beside the house—a Park Lane dream—
examines a Ceylon ruby for Lady B.,
orders up a gamelan orchestra.)

Raskolnikov,
stiff,
is wakened by Sonia "with the yellow ticket"
(a prostitute. Her father
is "surprisingly relaxed" about her calling),
she says:
"Get up! Come with me now!
Stand at the crossroads,
kiss the ground you soiled,
where you sinned,
then bow before all the world,
tell everyone aloud:
I am the murderer—
will you do that?
Will you come?"—
And he came.

Anyone who comforts another
is the mouth of Christ—

## STATISCHE GEDICHTE

Entwicklungsfremdheit
ist die Tiefe des Weisen,
Kinder und Kindeskinder
beunruhigen ihn nicht,
dringen nicht in ihn ein.

Richtungen vertreten,
Handeln,
Zu- und Abreisen
ist das Zeichen einer Welt,
die nicht klar sieht.
Vor meinem Fenster
– sagt der Weise –
liegt ein Tal,
darin sammeln sich die Schatten,
zwei Pappeln säumen einen Weg,
du weißt – wohin.

Perspektivismus
ist ein anderes Wort für seine Statik:
Linien anlegen,
sie weiterführen
nach Rankengesetz –

## STATIC POEMS

Aversion to progress
is profundity in the wise man,
children and grandchildren
don't bother him,
don't alarm him.

To represent a particular outlook,
to act,
to travel hither and yon
are all signs of a world
that doesn't see clearly.
In front of my window
—wise man says—
is a valley
where shadows pool,
two poplars mark a path,
leading you will know where to.

Another word for stasis
is perspective:
you draw lines,
they ramify
like a creeper—

*Ranken sprühen* –,
auch Schwärme, Krähen,
auswerfen in Winterrot von Frühhimmeln,

dann sinken lassen –

du weißt – für wen.

tendrils explode—
and they disburse crows in swarms
in the winter red of early dawns

then let them settle—

you will know—for whom.

**1949–1955**

## GEWISSE LEBENSABENDE

I

Du brauchst nicht immer die Kacheln zu scheuern, Hendrickje,
mein Auge trinkt sich selbst,
trinkt sich zu Ende –
aber an anderen Getränken mangelt es –
dort die Buddhastatue,
chinesischen Haingott,
gegen eine Kelle Hulstkamp,
bitte!

Nie etwas gemalt
in Frostweiß oder Schlittschuhläuferblau
oder dem irischen Grün,
aus dem der Purpur schimmert –
immer nur meine Eintönigkeit,
mein Schattenzwang –
nicht angenehm,
diesen Weg so deutlich zu verfolgen.

Größe – wo?
Ich nehme den Griffel
und gewisse Dinge stehn dann da

# EVENINGS OF CERTAIN LIVES

I

You don't need to be always scrubbing the tiles, Hendrickje,
my eye drinks itself,
drinks itself to death—
but other drink is in short supply—
the little Buddha there,
Chinese grove god
in exchange for a ladleful of Hulstkamp,
please!

Never painted anything
in frost white or ice-skater blue
or that Irish green
with the purple shimmering through—
always my own monotone,
my compulsion to shadows—
not pleasant
to pursue that path so clearly.

Greatness—how so?
I pick up the slate pencil and certain things appear
on paper or canvas

auf Papier, Leinwand
oder ähnlichem Zunder –
Resultat: Buddhabronze gegen Sprit –
aber Huldigungen unter Blattpflanzen,
Bankett der Pinselgilde –:
was fürs Genre –!

. . . Knarren,
Schäfchen, die quietschen,
Abziehbilder
flämisch, rubenisch
für die Enkelchen –!
(ebensolche Idioten –!)

Ah – Hulstkamp –
Wärmezentrum,
Farbenmittelpunkt,
mein Schattenbraun –
Bartstoppelfluidum um Herz und Auge –

II

Der Kamin raucht
– schneuzt sich der Schwan vom Avon –,
die Stubben sind naß,
klamme Nacht, Leere vermählt mit Zugluft –
Schluß mit den Gestalten,
übervölkert die Erde

or whatever the heck else—
Buddha hocked for booze—
but I draw the line at homages under ornamental plants,
banquet of the painters' guild—
something for the boardroom!

. . . Creaking,
little sheep squeaking, chromotypes
Flemish, Rubenesque—
for the grandchildren
(same idiots!)

Ah—Hulstkamp,
hits the spot,
midpoint of colors,
my shadow brown,
stubble aura around heart and eye—


II


The blocked chimney smokes
—the Swan of Avon blows his nose—
the tree stumps are sodden,
clammy night, emptiness mingled with draft—
enough characters,
the world is overpopulated as it is,

reichlicher Pfirsichfall, vier Rosenblüten
pro anno –
ausgestreut,
auf die Bretter geschoben
von dieser Hand,
faltig geworden
und mit erschlafften Adern!

Alle die Ophelias, Julias,
bekränzt, silbern, auch mörderisch –
alle die weichen Münder, die Seufzer,
die ich aus ihnen herausmanipulierte –
die ersten Aktricen längst Qualm,
Rost, ausgelaugt, Rattenpudding –
auch Herzens-Ariel bei den Elementen.

Die Epoche zieht sich den Bratenrock aus.
Diese Lord- und Läuseschädel,
ihre Gedankengänge,
die ich ins Extrem trieb –
meine Herren Geschichtsproduzenten
alles Kronen- und Szepteranalphabeten,
Großmächte des Weltraums
wie Fledermaus oder Papierdrachen!

Sir Goon schrieb neulich an mich:
„der Rest ist Schweigen": –
ich glaube, das ist von mir,
kann nur von mir sein,

plentiful peach-fall, four rosebuds
per annum—
asperged,
set to tread the boards
by this hand,
grown wrinkled
and with sluggish veins!

All those Juliets and Ophelias,
wreathed, silvered, sometimes murderous—
all the soft mouths, the sighs
I extracted from them—
the first actresses long since turned to smoke,
rust, leeched dry, rats' pudding—
heart's Ariel too with the elements.

The age takes off its frock coat.
These lousy skulls of lords,
their trains of thought
that I pushed into extremes—
my lords makers of history
all of them crowned and sceptered illiterates,
great powers of the cosmos—
yes, like so many bats or kites!

Sir Goon wrote to me lately:
"the rest is silence"—
I think that's one of mine,
could only be mine,

Dante tot – eine große Leere
zwischen den Jahrhunderten
bis zu meinen Wortschatzzitaten –

aber wenn sie fehlten,
der Plunder nie aufgeschlagen,
die Buden, die Schafotte, die Schellen
nie geklungen hätten –:
Lücken –?? Vielleicht Zahnlücken,
aber das große Affengebiß
mahlte weiter
seine Leere, vermählt mit Zugluft –
die Stubben sind naß
und der Butler schnarcht in Porterträumen.

Dante dead—lacuna
of centuries
to my alphabetical concordance—

what if they didn't exist,
the booty never found,
the booths, the scaffolds, the cymbals
never clashed—
gaps? Gap teeth maybe,
but the great monkey jaws
would grind on
emptiness, mingled with draft—
the tree stumps are sodden
and the butler snores in porter dreams.

## EIN SCHATTEN AN DER MAUER

Ein Schatten an der Mauer
von Ästen, bewegt im Mittagswind,
das ist genügend Erde
und hinsichtlich des Auges
genügend Teilnahme
am Himmelsspiel.

Wie weit willst du noch gehn? Verwehre
doch neuen Eindrücken
den drängenden Charakter –

stumm liegen,
die eigenen Felder sehn,
das ganze Rittergut,
besonders lange
auf Mohn verweilen,
dem unvergeßlichen,
weil er den Sommer trug –

wo ist er hin –?

## A SHADOW ON THE WALL

A shadow on the wall
boughs stirred by the noonday wind
that's enough earth
and for the eye
enough celestial participation.

How much further do you want to go? Refuse
the bossy insistence
of new impressions—

lie there still,
behold your own fields,
your estate,
dwelling especially
on the poppies,
unforgettable
because they transported the summer—

where did it go?

# FRAGMENTE

Fragmente,
Seelenauswürfe,
Blutgerinnsel des zwanzigsten Jahrhunderts –

Narben – gestörter Kreislauf der Schöpfungsfrühe,
die historischen Religionen von fünf Jahrhunderten zertrümmert,
die Wissenschaft: Risse im Parthenon,
Planck rann mit seiner Quantentheorie
zu Kepler und Kierkegaard neu getrübt zusammen –

aber Abende gab es, die gingen in den Farben
des Allvaters, lockeren, weitwallenden,
unumstößlich in ihrem Schweigen
geströmten Blaus,
Farbe der Introvertierten,
da sammelte man sich
die Hände auf das Knie gestützt
bäuerlich, einfach
und stillem Trunk ergeben
bei den Harmonikas der Knechte –

und andere
gehetzt von inneren Konvoluten,

## FRAGMENTS

Fragments,
soul flotsam,
coagulates of the twentieth century—

scars—breaks in flow from the dawn of creation,
the historical religions of five centuries in smithereens,
science: cracks in the Parthenon,
Planck blending with Kepler and Kierkegaard,
the fresh murk of his quantum theory—

but there were evenings robed in the colors
of the Almighty, loose, flowing,
incontrovertible in the silence
of their streaming blues,
color of introverts,
there I sat
hands spread on my knees
like a farmer,
quietly nursing my drink
while the laborers played harmonicas—

and others
are driven by inner whorls,

Wölbungsdrängen,
Stilbaukompressionen
oder Jagden nach Liebe.

Ausdruckskrisen und Anfälle von Erotik:
das ist der Mensch von heute,
das Innere ein Vakuum,
die Kontinuität der Persönlichkeit
wird gewahrt von den Anzügen,
die bei gutem Stoff zehn Jahre halten.

Der Rest Fragmente,
halbe Laute,
Melodienansätze aus Nachbarhäusern,
Negerspirituals
oder Ave Marias.

convolutes,

architectonic compressions

or amours.

Crises of expression and spasms of eros:

that's the man of today,

the inside a vacuum,

the continuity of personality

held together by his suit,

which with stout cloth might be good for ten years.

The rest fragments,

*mi-voix,*

snatches of melody from next door,

Negro spirituals

or Ave Marias.

## DENK DER VERGEBLICHEN

Wenn ein Verzweifeln
– der du doch große Stunden hattest
und sicher gingst und viele Beschenkungen
aus Rausch und Morgenröten und Wendungen,
unerwarteten,
dir pflegen konntest –
wenn ein Verzweifeln,
selbst mit Zerstörung und Endverglimmen
aus dem Unergründlichen
in seine Macht dich will:

denk der Vergeblichen,
die zarter Schläfe, inngewendeten Gesichts
in der Erinnerungen Treue,
die wenig Hoffnung ließen,
doch auch nach Blumen fragten
und still Verschwiegenes
mit einem Lächeln von wenig Ausdruck
in ihren kleinen Himmel hoben,
der bald verlöschen sollte.

# THINK OF THE UNSATISFIED ONES

When despair—
you who enjoyed great triumphs
and walked with confidence and the memory
of many gifts of delirium and dawns
and unexpected
turns—
when despair wants you in its grip,
and threatens you from some unfathomable depth
with destruction
and the guttering out of your flame:

then think of the unsatisfied ones,
with their migraine-prone temples and introverted dispositions,
loyal to a few memories
that held out little hope,
who still bought flowers
and with a smile of not much candle power
confided secret desires
to their small-scale heavens—
soon extinguished.

## SATZBAU

Alle haben den Himmel, die Liebe und das Grab,
damit wollen wir uns nicht befassen,
das ist für den Kulturkreis gesprochen und durchgearbeitet.
Was aber neu ist, ist die Frage nach dem Satzbau
und die ist dringend:
warum drücken wir etwas aus?

Warum reimen wir oder zeichnen ein Mädchen
direkt oder als Spiegelbild
oder stricheln auf eine Handbreit Büttenpapier
unzählige Pflanzen, Baumkronen, Mauern,
letztere als dicke Raupen mit Schildkrötenkopf
sich unheimlich niedrig hinziehend
in bestimmter Anordnung?

Überwältigend unbeantwortbar!
Honoraraussicht ist es nicht,
viele verhungern darüber. Nein,
es ist ein Antrieb in der Hand,
ferngesteuert, eine Gehirnlage,
vielleicht ein verspäteter Heilbringer oder Totemtier,
auf Kosten des Inhalts ein formaler Priapismus,

## SYNTAX

We all have the sky, and love, and the grave,
that's not at issue,
that's been chewed over and done to death in illustrated lecture
 series.
But what's new is the question of syntax
and that's urgent:
what makes us try to give expression to anything?

Why rhyme, or sketch a girl
either face-to-face or her mirror image,
or brush thicknesses of expensive laid paper
with innumerable plants, treetops, walls,
these last in the form of fat caterpillars with tortoise heads
creeping low to the ground
in fixed dispositions?

Overwhelmingly unanswerable!
Not the prospect of payment,
many starve in the process. No,
it's an impulse of the remote-controlled
hand, a condition of the brain,
perhaps a delayed Messiah or shamanic animal,
a priapism of form at the expense of content,

er wird vorübergehn,
aber heute ist der Satzbau
das Primäre.

„Die wenigen, die was davon erkannt" − (Goethe) −
wovon eigentlich?
Ich nehme an: vom Satzbau.

it will pass,
but today syntax
is primary.

"The few who understood anything about it?"—(Goethe)—
about what?
I imagine: about syntax.

# FINIS POLONIAE

Finis Poloniae –
eine Redewendung,
die abgesehn von ihrem historischen Inhalt
das Ende großer Reiche
bedeutet.

Verhexte Atmosphäre,
alles atmet beklommen,
Zwitterluft – falls sie Gedanken hätte,
wären es solche an uneuropäische Monsune
und gelbe Meere.

Das Große geht an sich selbst zugrunde,
spricht zu sich selbst den letzten Laut,
das fremde Lied, meistens verkannt,
gelegentlich geduldet –

Finis Poloniae –
vielleicht an einem Regentag, wenig beliebt,
doch für den vorliegenden Fall ein Geräusch von Glücken
und dann das Hornsolo,
im Anschluß eine Hortensie, die ruhigste der Blumen,
die bis November im Regen aushält,
leise auf die Grube.

## FINIS POLONIAE

Finis Poloniae—
a phrase / figure of speech,
that apart from its literal historical meaning
stands in for
the end of empires.

Charged atmosphere,
everything breathes damply,
epicene air—if it could think anything
it would think un-European things like monsoons
and yellow seas.

Greatness bears itself to death,
says its last words to itself,
a foreign-sounding swan song, generally misunderstood,
sometimes tolerated—

Finis Poloniae—
perhaps on a rainy day, bummer,
but in this instance a sound of happiness
followed by solo horn,
and then a hydrangea, most placid of flowers,
capable of standing out in the rain into November,
dropped softly into the grave.

# NOTTURNO

Im Nebenzimmer die Würfel auf den Holztisch,
benachbart ein Paar im Ansaugestadium,
mit einem Kastanienast auf dem Klavier tritt die Natur hinzu –
ein Milieu, das mich anspricht.

Da versinken die Denkprozesse,
die Seekrankheit, die einem tagsüber
die Brechzentren bearbeitet,
gehn unter in Alkohol und Nebulosem –
endlich Daseinsschwund und Seelenausglanz!

Auf Wogen liegen –
natürlich kann man untergehn,
aber das ist eine Zeitfrage –
doch Zeit – vor Ozeanen –?
Die waren vorher,
vor Bewußtsein und Empfängnis,
keiner fischte ihre Ungeheuer,
keiner litt tiefer als drei Meter
und das ist wenig.

## NOCTURNE

From the saloon bar the rattle of dice on a wooden tabletop,
beside you a couple at the anthropophagous stage,
a chestnut bough on the piano adds a natural touch,
all in all, my kind of place.

There, thought processes settle,
the nausea that exercised
your medulla oblongata all day
is allayed in a fog of alcohol—
at last soul fades and existence dims!

Treading water—
of course you might go down,
that's a matter of time—
and time—before oceans?
They were there first,
before consciousness and conception,
no one went angling for monsters,
no one suffered deeper than ten feet,
which if you think about it isn't so very much.

## GLADIOLEN

Ein Strauß Gladiolen
das ist bestimmt sehr schöpfungsdeutend,
fern von Blütengeweichel mit Fruchterhoffnung —:
langsam, haltbar, unirritiert,
großzügig, sicher der Königsträume.

Sonst die Natur- und Geisteswelt!
Dort die Wollherden:
Kleereste, mühselig, und daraus Schafsbröckel —
und hier die freundlichen Talente,
die Anna in den Mittelpunkt des Geschehens rücken,
sie läutern und einen Ausweg wissen!

Hier ist kein Ausweg:
Da sein — fallen —,
nicht die Tage zählen —
Vollendung
schön, böse oder zerrissen.

# GLADIOLI

A bunch of glads,
certainly highly emblematic of creation,
remote from frills of working blossom with hope of fruit—
slow, durable, placid,
generous, sure of kingly dreams.

All else is natural world and intellect!
Over there the mutton herds:
strenuous ends of clover and daggy sheep—
here friendly talents,
pushing Anna to the center of attention,
explaining her, finding a solution!

The glads offer no solution:
being—falling—
you mustn't count the days—
fulfillment
livid, tattered, or beautiful.

# RESTAURANT

Der Herr drüben bestellt sich noch ein Bier,
das ist mir angenehm, dann brauche ich mir keinen Vorwurf
   zu machen,
daß ich auch gelegentlich einen zische.
Man denkt immer gleich, man ist süchtig,
in einer amerikanischen Zeitschrift las ich sogar,
jede Zigarette verkürze das Leben um sechsunddreißig Minuten,
das glaube ich nicht, vermutlich steht die Coca-Cola-Industrie
oder eine Kaugummifabrik hinter dem Artikel.

Ein normales Leben, ein normaler Tod
das ist auch nichts. Auch ein normales Leben
führt zu einem kranken Tod. Überhaupt hat der Tod
mit Gesundheit und Krankheit nichts zu tun,
er bedient sich ihrer zu seinem Zwecke.

Wie meinen Sie das: der Tod hat mit Krankheit nichts zu tun?
Ich meine das so: viele erkranken, ohne zu sterben,
also liegt hier noch etwas anderes vor,
ein Fragwürdigkeitsfragment,
ein Unsicherheitsfaktor,
er ist nicht so klar umrissen,
hat auch keine Hippe,
beobachtet, sieht um die Ecke, hält sich sogar zurück
und ist musikalisch in einer anderen Melodie.

## RESTAURANT

The gentleman over there orders another pint,
well, that's nice, then I don't need to worry
if I have another myself in due course.
Trouble is, one straightaway thinks one is addicted,
I even read in an American magazine
that every cigarette you smoke takes thirty-six minutes off your
     life;
I don't believe that, presumably it's the chewing-gum industry
that's behind that, or Coca-Cola.

A normal life and a normal death—
I don't know what they're good for. Even a normal life
ends in an unhealthy death. Altogether death
doesn't have a lot to do with health and sickness,
it merely uses them for its own purposes.

What do you mean, death doesn't have a lot to do with sickness?
I mean this: a lot of people get sick without dying,
so what we have before us is something different,
the introduction of a variable,
a source of uncertainty,
not an open-and-shut case,
not the grim reaper mounted on a bag of bones,
but something that observes, sees round corners, exercises restraint,
and musically plays a different tune.

## BLAUE STUNDE

### I

Ich trete in die dunkelblaue Stunde –
da ist der Flur, die Kette schließt sich zu
und nun im Raum ein Rot auf einem Munde
und eine Schale später Rosen – Du!

Wir wissen beide, jene Worte,
die jeder oft zu anderen sprach und trug,
sind zwischen uns wie nichts und fehl am Orte:
dies ist das Ganze und der letzte Zug.

Das Schweigende ist so weit vorgeschritten
und füllt den Raum und denkt sich selber zu
die Stunde – nichts gehofft und nichts gelitten –
mit ihrer Schale später Rosen – Du.

### II

Dein Haupt verfließt, ist weiß und will sich hüten,
indessen sammelt sich auf deinem Mund
die ganze Lust, der Purpur und die Blüten
aus deinem angeströmten Ahnengrund.

# BLUE HOUR

I

I enter the deep blue hour—
here is the landing, the chain shuts behind
and now in the room only carmine on a mouth
and a bowl of late roses—you!

We both know, those words
that we both spoke and often offered others
are of no account and out of place between us:
this is everything and endgame.

Silence has advanced so far
it fills the room and seals it shut
the hour—nothing hoped and nothing suffered—
with its bowl of late roses—you.

II

Your face blurs, is white, and fragile,
meanwhile there collects on your mouth
all of desire, the purple and the blossoms
from some ancestral flotsam stock.

Du bist so weiß, man denkt, du wirst zerfallen
vor lauter Schnee, vor lauter Blütenlos,
todweiße Rosen Glied für Glied – Korallen
nur auf den Lippen, schwer und wundengroß.

Du bist so weich, du gibst von etwas Kunde,
von einem Glück aus Sinken und Gefahr
in einer blauen, dunkelblauen Stunde
und wenn sie ging, weiß keiner, ob sie war.


III

Ich frage dich, du bist doch eines andern,
was trägst du mir die späten Rosen zu?
Du sagst, die Träume gehn, die Stunden wandern,
was ist das alles: er und ich und du?

„Was sich erhebt, das will auch wieder enden,
was sich erlebt – wer weiß denn das genau,
die Kette schließt, man schweigt in diesen Wänden
und dort die Weite, hoch und dunkelblau.“

You are so pale, I think you might founder
in a snowdrift, in unblooming
deathly white roses, one by one—coral
only on your lips, heavy and like a wound.

You are so soft, you portend something
of happiness, of submersion and danger
in a blue, a deep blue hour
and when it's gone, no one knows if it was.


III

I remind you, you are another's,
what are you doing bearing me these late roses?
You say dreams bleach, hours wander,
what is all this: he and I and you?

"What arises and arouses, it all comes to an end,
what happens—who exactly knows,
the chain falls shut, we are silent in these walls,
and outside is all of space, lofty and dark blue."

## IDEELLES WEITERLEBEN?

Bald
ein abgesägter, überholter
früh oder auch spät verstorbener Mann,
von dem man spricht wie von einer Sängerin
mit ausgesungenem Sopran
oder vom kleinen Hölty mit seinen paar Versen –
noch weniger: Durchschnitt,
nie geflogen,
keinen Borgward gefahren –
Zehnpfennigstücke für die Tram,
im Höchstfall Umsteiger.

Dabei ging täglich so viel bei dir durch
introvertiert, extrovertiert,
Nahrungssorgen, Ehewidrigkeit, Steuermoral –
mit allem mußtest du dich befassen,
ein gerüttelt Maß von Leben in mancherlei Gestalt.

Auf einer Karte aus Antibes,
die ich heute erhielt,
ragt eine Burg in die Méditerranée,
eine fanatische Sache:
südlich, meerisch, schneeig, am Rande hochgebirgig –

## THEORETICAL AFTERLIFE?

Soon through,
out of time,
a man prematurely or otherwise deceased,
of whom people speak the way they speak of a singer
with a clapped-out soprano
or little Hölty with his few ditties—
less than that: just par,
never went up in a plane,
never took the wheel of a Borgward—
a dime for the streetcar,
at most, transfer.

But so much went by you every day,
introverted, extroverted,
existential worries, marital strife, tax issues—
with all of that you had to concern yourself,
a pile of life in variegated forms.

On a postcard from Antibes
that arrived today
a castle soars into the Med,
a freakish object:
the south, the sea, snowcapped mountains on the periphery—

Jahrhunderte, dramatisiert,
ragen, ruhen, glänzen, firnen, strotzen
sich in die Aufnahme –
nichts von alledem bei dir,
keine Ingredienzien zu einer Ansichtskarte –
Zehnpfennigstücke für die Tram,
Umsteiger,
und schnell die obenerwähnte Wortprägung:
überholt.

a dramatization of centuries
soars, rests, shines, glamors, obtrudes
into the snap—
none of all that *chez toi,*
not so much as the wherewithal for a postcard—
a dime for the streetcar,
transfer,
and soon enough the words above:
out of time.

## STILLEBEN

Wenn alles abgeblättert daliegt
Gedanken, Stimmungen, Duette
abgeschilfert – hautlos daliegt,
kein Stanniol – und das Abgehäutete
– alle Felle fortgeschwommen –
blutiger Bindehaut ins Stumme äugt –:
was ist das?

Die Frage der Fragen! Aber kein Besinnlicher
fragt sie mehr –
Renaissancereminiszenzen,
Barocküberladungen,
Schloßmuseen –

nur keine weiteren Bohrungen,
doch kein Grundwasser,
die Brunnen dunkel,
die Stile erschöpft –

die Zeit hat etwas Stilles bekommen,
die Stunde atmet,
über einem Krug,
es ist spät, die Schläge verteilt

## STILL LIFE

When everything lies there in fallen heaps
thoughts, moods, duets
—lies there despoiled
without tinfoil—and the scraped membrane
—all the layers washed away—
of the bloody conjunctiva stares into silence—
what's left?

The sixty-four-thousand-dollar question! But who in his senses
asks it anymore—
Renaissance reminiscences,
Baroque overlay,
castle museums—

an end to drilling,
but still no groundwater,
the wells dark,
the styles exhausted—

time has acquired a stillness,
the hour breathes
over a wine jug,
it's late, the last blows have been traded,

noch ein wenig Clinch und Halten,
Gong – ich verschenke die Welt
wem sie genügt, soll sich erfreun:

der Spieler soll nicht ernst werden
der Trinker nicht in die Gobi gehn,
auch eine Dame mit Augenglas
erhebt Anspruch auf ihr Glück:
sie soll es haben –

still ruht der See,
vergißmeinnichtumsäumt,
und die Ottern lachen.

a clinch and a hang on the ropes
before the bell—I give the world
to anyone who wants it, let them be happy:

the jester's not to turn serious
the drinker's not to wander into the Gobi Desert
even a lady with lorgnette
entertains aspirations to happiness:
well, good luck to her—

the lake rests at ease
rimmed with forget-me-nots,
adders laugh.

# BEGEGNUNGEN

Welche Begegnungen in diesen Tagen
reif, golden, pfirsichrund,
wo immer noch die Sonnenbräute (Helenium)
wirksame Farben in den Garten tragen –
von Alter schwer,
von Alter leicht,
wo selbst die Träne sich auf den Rücken klopft:
„nur halb so schlimm und nicht mehr lange" –

Begegnungen, zum Beispiel Dämmerstunde,
l'heure bleue, die Schöpfung zittert von Samba,
die Herren legen die Hände
zwischen die Schulterblätter der Dame,
von Fiesole bis La Paz
nun Sinnlichkeit und Freude global im Schwange –

oder die Lieder vom Ohio,
die hängen dort in den Bäumen,
im Schilfrohr und in den Träumen
der Jugend, die in das Leben zieht –
wie lange –?

## ENCOUNTERS

Such encounters these days
ripe, golden, peach-curved,
where the sun's brides (Helenium)
still carry effective colors into the garden—
heavy with age /
light with age,
where even the teardrop says: "Chin up!
It's not so bad, and not long to go!"—

Encounters, for instance dusk,
*l'heure bleue*, creation trembles with samba,
the gentleman lays his hand
between his partner's shoulder blades,
all over the world from Fiesole to La Paz
sensuality and joy—

or the songs of the Ohio River,
hanging in the trees,
in reeds and dreams
of youth, on the cusp of life—
how soon, and how long—?

Das Gelb des Strandes und das Blau der Nacht
und am Korallenriff das Weiß der Jacht,
was je an Traum und Mythen in dir war,
erblickst du vom Hotel in Denpasar –

Begegnungen, die ohne Zentrum sind,
sie haben keinen Vater und kein Kind,
Begegnungen von einer Pfirsichwange
mit einer Sonnenbraut im Himmelsgange,
Begegnungen – das Frühe und das Spät,
ein Sein, das dann an andere übergeht.

Yellow of strand and blue of night
and on the coral reef the white yacht,
whatever was in you of dream and myth,
you behold from your hotel window in Denpasar—

encounters lacking a center,
no father and no child,
encounters of a peachy complexion
with a sun's bride in heaven's corridor,
encounters—the early and the late,
the torch of existence passes from hand to hand.

## EINE HYMNE

Mit jener Eigenschaft der großen Puncher:
Schläge hinnehmen können
stehn,

Feuerwasser in der Kehle gurgeln
sub- und supraatomar
dem Rausch begegnet sein,
Sandalen
am Krater lassen wie Empedokles
und dann hinab,

nicht sagen: Wiederkehr
nicht denken: halb und halb,
Maulwurfshügel freigeben
wenn Zwerge sich vergrößern wollen,
allroundgetafelt bei sich selbst
unteilbar
und auch den Sieg verschenken können –

eine Hymne solchem Mann.

## HYMN

That quality of the great boxers
to be able to stand there
and take shots,

gargle with firewater,
encounter intoxication
at sub- and supra-atomic levels,
to leave one's sandals at the crater's lip
like Empedocles, and descend,

not say: I'll be back,
not think: fifty-fifty,
to vacate molehills
when dwarves want space to grow,
to dine alone,
indivisible,
and able to renounce your victory—

a hymn to that man.

## WAS SCHLIMM IST

Wenn man kein Englisch kann,
von einem guten englischen Kriminalroman zu hören,
der nicht ins Deutsche übersetzt ist.

Bei Hitze ein Bier sehn,
das man nicht bezahlen kann.

Einen neuen Gedanken haben,
den man nicht in einen Hölderlinvers einwickeln kann,
wie es die Professoren tun.

Nachts auf Reisen Wellen schlagen hören
und sich sagen, daß sie das immer tun.

Sehr schlimm: eingeladen sein,
wenn zu Hause die Räume stiller,
der Café besser
und keine Unterhaltung nötig ist.

Am schlimmsten:
nicht im Sommer sterben,
wenn alles hell ist
und die Erde für Spaten leicht.

## WHAT'S BAD

Not reading English,
and hearing about a new English thriller
that hasn't been translated.

Seeing a cold beer when it's hot out,
and not being able to afford it.

Having an idea
that you can't encapsulate in a line of Hölderlin,
the way the professors do.

Hearing the waves beat against the shore on holiday at night,
and telling yourself it's what they always do.

Very bad: being invited out,
when your own room at home is quieter,
the coffee is better,
and you don't have to make small talk.

And worst of all:
not to die in summer,
when the days are long
and the earth yields easily to the spade.

# AUSSENMINISTER

Aufs Ganze gerichtet
sind die Völker eine Messe wert,
aber im einzelnen: laßt die Trompete zu der Pauke sprechen,
jetzt trinkt der König Hamlet zu –
wunderbarer Aufzug,
doch die Degenspitze vergiftet.

„Iswolski lachte."
Zitate zur Hand, Bonmots in der Kiepe,
hier kühl, dort chaleureux, Peace and Goodwill,
lieber mal eine Flöte zuviel,
die Shake-hands Wittes in Portsmouth (1905)
waren Rekord, aber der Friede wurde günstiger.

Vorm Parlament – das ist keineswegs Schaumschlägerei,
hat Methode wie Sanskrit oder Kernphysik,
enormes Labor: Referenten, Nachrichtendienst, Empirie,
auch Charakter muß man durchfühlen,
im Ernst: Charakter haben die Hochgekommenen ganz bestimmt,
nicht wegen etwaiger Prozesse,
sondern er ist ihr moralischer Sex-Appeal –
allerdings: was ist der Staat?
„Ein Seiendes unter Seienden",
sagte schon Plato.

# FOREIGN MINISTERS

Considered as a whole,
the nations are worth a Mass,
but individually: let trumpet speak to drum,
the King drinks to Hamlet—
a terrific scene,
but the foils are poisoned.

"Izwolski laughed."
Quotes at his fingertips, bons mots up his sleeve,
now frosty, now charming, peace and goodwill,
better one toot on the flute too many,
Count Witte's glad-handing in Portsmouth (1905)
broke all records, but the terms were more favorable.

To parliament—by no means bunkum,
there's a method to it just as there is in Sanskrit or particle physics,
and a huge staff besides: researchers, press office, spear-carriers,
and you have to be able to feel the man's character
through the whole: seriously, highfliers have it,
not through some processes or other,
but the moral equivalent of sex appeal—
and then: what is a state anyway?
The actuality of the ethical idea,
according to Plato.

„Zwiespalt zwischen der öffentlichen
und der eigentlichen Meinung" (Keynes). Opalisieren!
Man lebt zwischen les hauts et les bas,
erst Oberpräsident, dann kleiner Balkanposten, schließlich Chef,
dann ein neues Revirement,
und man geht auf seine Güter.
Leicht gesagt: verkehrte Politik.
Wann verkehrt? Heute? Nach zehn Jahren? Nach einem
    Jahrhundert?


Mésalliancen, Verrat, Intrigen,
alles geht zu unseren Lasten,
man soll das Ölzeug anziehn,
bevor man auf Fahrt geht,
beobachten, ob die Adler rechts oder links fliegen,
die heiligen Hühner das Futter verweigern.
Als Hannibal mit seinen Elefanten über den Simplon zog,
war alles in Ordnung,
als später Karthago fiel,
weinte Salambo.


Sozialismus – Kapitalismus –: wenn die Rebe wächst
und die Volkswirtschaft verarbeitet ihren Saft
dank außerordentlicher Erfindungen und Manipulationen
zu Mousseux – dann muß man ihn wohl auch trinken?
Oder soll man die Kelten verurteilen,
weil sie den massilischen Stock
tauschweise nach Gallien trugen –
damit würde man ja jeden zeitlichen Verlauf
und die ganze Kulturausbreitung verdammen.

"Dichotomy between public
and private opinion" (Keynes). Opalesce!
You live in the divide between the high-ups and the others,
first COO, then obscure posting in the Balkans, finally top dog,
then a reshuffle,
and you retire to your estate.
Easily said: mistaken political direction.
Mistaken when? Today? In ten years? Next century?

Mésalliances, treachery, intrigues,
all at our expense,
be sure you slip on a sou'wester
before you go out,
check whether the eagles are flying left or right,
if the sacred pullets are off their feed.
When Hannibal came over the Simplon with his elephants,
everything looked plain sailing;
later, when Carthage fell,
Salammbô wept.

Socialism—Capitalism—if the grape grows,
and the national economy converts its juice
by means of certain extraordinary inventions and manipulations
to *mousseux*—then someone has to drink it, no?
Or should we blame the Celts
for carrying off the Massilian stock
back to Gaul with them by way of exchange—
that would be to condemn history, progress,
and the spread of cultures.

„Die Außenminister kamen in einer zweistündigen Besprechung
zu einem vorläufigen Ergebnis"
(Öl- und Pipelinefragen),
drei trugen Cutaway,
einer einen Burnus.

"At the end of a two-hour meeting,
the foreign ministers came to a provisional agreement"
(oil and pipeline questions),
three wore tails,
one was in a burnoose.

## TRAUM

„Haltestelle und Lebensbahn"
las ich gerade in der Zeitung
als zwei Gestalten aus dem Wald traten
längst Verstorbene
beide mit steifem Hut und Rucksack

nicht gleichzeitig
an zwei Tagen hintereinander
alte Bekannte, ja Verwandte
ich fragte, wohin sie
zu dieser ungewohnten Lebens- beziehungsweise Sterbensstunde
    wollten
aber sie blickten nur unwirsch auf
und einer deutete an, er werde
mehrere Wochen bei einem Apotheker verbringen.

Beide hielten zurück
ihre Züge deuteten auf:
Querverbindungen
Überraschungen
inzwischen Verändertes

ich war so klug wie vorher
wie vor Haltestelle und Lebensbahn.

## DREAM

I had just read "Bus Stop
and Biography" in the newspaper
when two figures emerged from the forest
both long dead,
kitted out with top hats and rucksacks

not at the same time
but on two successive days
old acquaintances, yes, family members
I asked them where they were going at this unwonted hour of
    life or, rather, death,
but they only looked up crossly
and one of them remarked
he was going to spend several weeks with an apothecary.

A reserved pair,
their features indicated
cross-connections
surprises
changes of plan

I knew as little as before,
as before bus stop and biography.

# VERZWEIFLUNG

I

Was du in Drogerien sprachst
beim Einkauf von Mitteln
oder mit deinem Schneider
außerhalb des Maßgeschäftlichen –
was für ein Nonsens diese Gesprächsfetzen,
warst du da etwa drin?

Morgens – noch etwas erschöpft
von den Aufstehmanipulationen –
leicht hingeplappert, um nicht gleich wieder hinauszugehn,
dies und jenes, Zeitgeschichtliches,
Grundsätzliches, alles durcheinander –
Grundsätzliches ist übrigens gut!
Wo sitzt das denn bei dir? Im Magen? Wie lange?
Was ist das überhaupt? Triebfonds, Hoffnungszement,
    Wirtschaftskalkül –
jedenfalls etwas ungemein Prekäres!

Alles zusammengerechnet
aus Morgen- und Tagesstunden
in Zivil und Uniform

# DESPAIR

I

Things you said in drugstores
when buying painkillers
or at your tailor's
apart from details of measurements or cut—
*brouillons* of chitchat,
in what way did they ever express you?

In the morning—still shattered
from the palaver of getting up—
things babbled, so as not to stagger off in silence,
this and that, bits of news,
general truths, all mixed up—
the general truths were always your forte!
Where is the seat of that in you? In your gut? Since when?
And what is it anyway? Source of instinct, cement of optimism,
    economic speculation—
certainly something incredibly flimsy!

All of it totted up
from morning and nighttime hours,
in civvies and in uniform

erbricht sich rückblickend vor Überflüssigkeit,
toten Lauten, Hohlechos
und Überhaupt-mit-nichts-Zusammensein –

oder beginnt hier die menschliche Gemeinschaft?


II

Alle die Verschlagenheiten,
das Grinsen ins Gesicht von jemandem,
den du dir erhalten willst,
aber auch nicht die Wahrheit über dich sagen,
nicht fühlen lassen das Rohe, das Schielen, den Verrat,
vor allem, weil du selber gar nicht weißt,
was Schielen und Verrat eigentlich ist,
dies ganze Gewebe aus List, Unzucht und Halbtränen –

Kürten – seinerzeit in Düsseldorf –
von sieben bis neun abends Lustmörder,
im übrigen Kegelbruder und Familienvater
war das nicht vollsinnig
und der Pithekanthropus erectus?

Kulturkreise hinten und vorn,
Morgen-, Mittag- und Abendländer,
Höhlenzeichnungen, dicke Madonnen,
Hermaphroditengeschlinge,
Sodomiterei als Rasensport –

makes you vomit with its superfluousness
as you look back, dead words, hollow sounds,
no connection with anything—

or is it here that human fellowship begins?


II


All the ruses,
the shameless grinning in the face of someone
you want on your side,
without telling them the truth about you,
without revealing the coarseness, the ogling, the betrayal,
mainly because you don't really know
what ogling and betrayal are,
that whole tissue of cunning, unmannerliness, and semi-tears.—

Kürten in Düsseldorf—
from 7 till 9 engaged in rape and murder,
but all the rest of the time bowling club member and paterfamilias—
wasn't that reasonable
and in keeping with *Pithecanthropus erectus?*

Culture clubs may come and go,
Orient, Occident, and accident,
cave drawings, feisty Madonnas,
hermaphroditic equipment,
plein air sodomy—

alles hin und her und keiner sinnt es
bis zu den Göttern,
bis zu Ende.

Lächle, nimm duftende Seife,
eh du zu der Geliebten eilst
und vorm Rasieren einfetten,
das schönt die Haut.


III

Sprich zu dir selbst, dann sprichst du zu den Dingen
und von den Dingen, die so bitter sind,
ein anderes Gespräch wird nie gelingen,
den Tod trägt beides, beides endet blind.

Hier singt der Osten und hier trinkt der Westen,
aus offenen Früchten rinnt es und vom Schaft
der Palmen, Gummibäume und in Resten
träuft auch die Orchidee den Seltsamsaft.

Du überall, du allem nochmals offen,
die letzte Stunde und du steigst und steigst,
dann noch ein Lied, und wunderbar getroffen
sinkst du hinüber, weißt das Sein und schweigst.

all comes and goes and no one thinks it through
to the gods,
to the finish.

So smile, use scented soap
when you run to your mistress,
and grease your skin before you shave;
that keeps it supple.


III


When you talk to yourself, you talk to the things
and of the things, that are so bitter,
no other conversation is possible,
both bear death, both end blind.

Here the East sings and the West sinks pints,
fruit explodes with ripeness,
ooze from palm and gum tree
even the orchid runs with individual juice.

You all over, you once again open to all,
the final hour, and you soar and soar,
then one more song, and beautifully hit,
you sink, you know existence, and you hold your peace.

## „DER BROADWAY SINGT UND TANZT"

*Eine magnifique Reportage!*

1) Das Debüt der Negersängerin als Wahrsagerin
Ulrika im Maskenball,
bisher nur als Lieder- und Arienvirtuosin bekannt,
nun mit großem Orchester und berühmten Stimmen:
„glückte vollendet".

2) Vorfälle, dramatisiert: alles Kompromißler,
nur bei einem einzigen der Versuch, „gegen die Mühle
der Mehrheitsmeinung"
„die Wahrheit an den Tag zu bringen"
(großartig – aber siehe Pilatus).

3) Kaiserinmutter und Prinzessin Irina:
ein „mit fast unerträglicher innerer (!) Spannung
geladenes Duell",
drei Hochstapler kommen noch dazu –
(wenn das nicht prima ist!)

4) Noah und seine Familie – die ganze Sintflut,
die Fahrt der Arche bis zum Aufstoßen,
„der bekannte Patriarch"

## "BROADWAY SINGS AND DANCES"

*A Magnifique Reportage!*

1. The debut of the black singer
(hitherto known for her work in lieder and aria)
as the fortune-teller Ulrica in *The Masked Ball*,
now with full-scale orchestral backing and famous voices:
"a resounding triumph."

2. Incidents, dramatized: trimmers the lot of them,
just one instance of "trying
to bring truth to light"
"in the teeth of majority opinion"
(splendid—but see also Pontius Pilate).

3. Dowager Empress and the Princess Irina:
a contest fraught with almost unbearable inner (!)
tension,
then three con men show up
(an unbeatable formula!).

4. Noah and his brood—the whole story of the Flood
the voyage of the Ark till landfall,
the "celebrated patriarch"

eine „im tiefsten Sinne spannende Haltung"
„fast betäubend",
dem Komponisten wurden die Songs
per Telefon von New York nach St. Moritz vorgespielt
(allerlei! Arche-Noah-Songs!)

Dagegen unser Europa! Vielleicht Urgrund der Seele;
aber viel Nonsens, Salbader:
„Die Wahrheit", Lebenswerk, 500 Seiten –
so lang kann die Wahrheit doch gar nicht sein!
oder:
„Das Denkerische über das Denken",
das ist bestimmt nicht so betäubend
wie Broadway-Noah

Immer: Grundriß!

Kinder! Kinder!

his attitude "in every sense profound,"
"literally stunning,"
the songs were played to the lyricist
by phone from New York to St. Moritz
(gee willikers! Noah's Ark songs!)

As against our Europe! Ur-stomping-ground of the spirit as may be,
but so much pretentious twaddle:
"The Truth," a life's work, 500 pages—
the truth can't be that long!
Or:
"Philosophy for Philosophers,"
whatever it is it won't be so "literally stunning"
as Noah on Broadway.

Remember: sketch!

Boy, oh boy!

# IMPROMPTU

Im Radio sang einer
„In der Drosselgaß zu Rüdesheim" –
ich war erschlagen:
Drosseln, das ist doch wohl ein Frühlingstag,
wer weiß, was über die Mauern hing,
quoll, zwitscherte, sicher Hellgrünes –
das Herz stieg auf, noch nicht das alte jetzt
das junge noch, nach einem Wandertag,
berauscht und müde.

Auch wer nie Wein trank,
hier gab man Goldenes an seinen Gaumen,
schlug sich den Staub vom Rock,
dann auf ein Lager
den Rucksack unter den Kopf,
die beide nichts enthielten
als für des nächsten Tags
Gelegenheiten.

Ein Paar Schuhe. Ein Musensohn.
Damals war Liliencron mein Gott,
ich schrieb ihm eine Ansichtskarte.

# IMPROMPTU

On the radio someone was singing
"Die Drosselgass' zu Rüdesheim"—
I was stunned:
thrushes, that seems to imply a spring day,
who knows what dangling over the walls,
unbundling, twittering, something in light green for sure—
my heart leapt, not the old one of today
but the young one, tired and exhilarated
at the end of a day's hike.

Even if you didn't drink wine,
you poured yourself something golden in a glass,
brushed the dust from your coat,
and flopped down on a pallet,
with your rucksack jammed under your head,
neither of them with anything in them
except what you needed
for the morrow.

A pair of shoes. A son of the Muses.
Back then, Liliencron was my God,
and I wrote him a postcard.

## BAUXIT

Diese Woche war ziemlich teuer,
sagen wir: vierhundert Mark,
aber sie hatte zauberhafte Augenblicke,
sublime, innerliche, seidenweiche
mit Strömen von berauschter Transzendenz.

Ich betrachte oft mit Interesse
die rechte Hand der Herren:
es ist die Hand, die eröffnet,
meistens lohnt es sich kaum,
aber die Fälle, deren man sich erinnert,
sind die Glücke der tiefaufatmenden
weißen weichen Kastanienblüte,
die im Mai uns segnet.

Von Nebentischen hört man oft: „Wir Grossisten",
„Herr Kraft, was nützen Kunden,
die die Solawechsel nicht zahlen",
„Dreizehn Mark fünfzig als Monatsrate":
die ganze Welt ist voll von solchen Worten.
Demgegenüber die Inkassos des Himmels,
verderblich vielleicht, in gewissem Sinne sträflich,
aber man lag herum, abgeschabt, ausverkauft, richtiger Verschleiß

## BAUXITE

I spent a lot of money this week,
almost four hundred marks,
but it did make possible some magical moments,
sublime, interior, silk-soft,
with flows of intoxicating transcendence.

I often study
an individual's right hand:
it's the hand that opens,
usually it's not worth the candle,
but the times that you remember
are the blisses of the deeply breathing
soft white chestnut flowers
that are a blessing in May.

From other tables one hears: "We're tutti players,"
or "Herr Kraft, what good are customers
who don't pay their promissory notes,"
or "The monthly installments are thirteen-fifty":
the world is full of such sayings.
And confronting them the encashments of heaven,
ruinous perhaps, in a certain sense criminal,
but you were lying around shop-soiled, grubby, sale item,

und nun für vierhundert Mark
Quaderrisse
Felsensprengungen
die Adern leuchten
pures Gold
Bauxit

eine ganze Woche, wo, des Himmels: „Wir Grossisten"

and now for four hundred marks
cracks in the rocks
detonations
the veins shimmer
with pure gold
bauxite—

an entire week for heaven's "tutti players"

## NUR NOCH FLÜCHTIG ALLES

Nur noch flüchtig alles,
kein Orplid, keine Bleibe,
Gestalten, Ungestalten
abrupte
mit Verkürzung.

Serge Rubinstein
zwei Millionen Dollar
auf schmale, breite, strenge
zahnschöne, hell- und schmieräugige
Ladies, Stepgirls, Barvamps
umgelegt,
das Leukoplast über dem Rüssel,
als er erwürgt wurde,
auf Fingerabdrücke untersucht,
ergab keine Anhaltspunkte.

Nur noch flüchtig alles –
nun die Anden:
Ur, verrunzelt,
nichts für Geodäten,
a-nousisch
a-musisch
Randwelt

## ONLY FLEETING NOW

Only fleeting now,
no Orplid, nowhere permanent,
figures, disfigurements
abrupt,
curtailed.

Serge Rubinstein
sank
two million dollars
in skinny, voluptuous, strict,
blue- and murky-eyed
ladies, hoofers, dentists' receptionists and vamps,
the piece of sticking plaster on his conk
when he was strangled
was scanned for fingerprints,
but provided no leads.

Only fleeting now—
it's the turn of the Andes:
aboriginal, wrinkled,
nothing for geodesists,
no *nous*
no Muse
edge world

fortsehn –
gebt Steckrüben!
gebt Knollenhumus!

gebt Gottesliter,
Höllenyards,
gebt Rillen
einzuhalten,
aufzuhalten
*einnisten* möchte man schreien –
nichts –
gebt Rillen!

Nur noch flüchtig alles
Neuralgien morgens,
Halluzinationen abends
angelehnt an Trunk und Zigaretten

abgeschlossene Gene,
erstarrte Chromosomen,
noch etwas schwitzende Hüfte
bei Boogie-Woogie,
nach Heimkehr dann die Hose in den Bügel.

Wo schließt sich was,
wo leuchtet etwas ferne,
nichts von Orplid –
Kulturkreis:
Zahl Pi mit Seiltricks!

look further—
yields beets!
yields potato fields!

yields liters of God,
yards of hell,
yields grooves
to record
to arrest
to nest in, one would fain cry—
nothing—
yields grooves!

Only fleeting now
neuralgia in the morning
hallucinations at night
propped on alcohol and cigarettes

occluded genes
frozen chromosomes,
the crutch perspires a little
to the boogie-woogie,
then the pants are returned to their press.

Where is anything resolved,
where does anything shine from afar,
no Orplid—
culture club:
Pye plus ropetricks!

## VERLIESS DAS HAUS –

### I

Verließ das Haus, verzehrt, er litt so sehr,
so viele Jahre Mensch, mit Zwischendingen,
trotz Teilerfolg im Geistesringen
war keiner von olympischem Gewähr.

So ging er langsam durch die Rêverie
des späten Herbsttags, kaum zu unterscheiden
von einem Frühlingstag mit jungen Weiden
und einem Kahlschlag, wo der Häher schrie.

So träumerisch von Dingen überspielt,
die die Natur in Lenken und Verwalten
entfernter Kreise – jüngeren und alten –
als unaufhebbar einer Ordnung fühlt –:

So trank er denn den Schnaps und nahm die Tracht
Wurstsuppe, donnerstags umsonst gereichte
an jeden Gast, und fand das angegleichte
Olympische von Lust und Leidensmacht.

## LEFT THE HOUSE

I

Left the house shattered, it hurt so bad,
so many years as a man, compromise,
mixed success in intellectual combat
but he was never anyone of Olympian allure.

He walked slowly through the dreamscape
of the late autumn day, barely distinguishable
from early spring, with young willows
and a patch of waste ground where blue jays screamed.

Dreamy exposure to phenomena
that to nature in its administration
of various cycles—young and old alike—
are inseparably part of a single order—:

so he drank his gin and accepted a dish
of sausage soup (free on Thursdays
with a beverage), and so found the Olympian balance
of sorrow and pleasure.

II

Er hatte etwas auf der Bank gelesen
und in der letzten Rosen Grau gesehn,
es waren keine Stämme, Buschwerkwesen,
gelichtet schon von Fall und Untergehn.

Nun sank das Buch. Es war ein Tag wie alle
und Menschen auch wie alle im Revier,
das würde weiter sein, in jedem Falle
blieb dies Gemisch von Tod und Lachen hier.

Schon ein Geruch kann mancherlei entkräften,
auch kleine Blumen sind der Zeder nah –
dann ging er weiter und in Pelzgeschäften
lag manches Warme für den Winter da.

III

Ganz schön – gewiß – für Schnaps und eine Weile
im Park am Mittag, wenn die Sonne scheint,
doch wenn der Hauswirt kommt, gewisse Teile
der Steuer fehlen und die Freundin weint?

Verzehrt: wie weit darfst du dein Ich betreiben,
Absonderliches als verbindlich sehn?
Verzehrt: wie weit mußt du im Genre bleiben –
so weit wie Ludwig Richters Bilder gehn?

## II

He had been reading on the park bench
and stared into the gray of the last roses,
there were no titans, just shrubs
thinned out by fall.

He set aside his book. It was a day like any other
and the people were like all people in the area,
that was how it would always be, at least
this mixture of death and laughter would persist.

A scent is enough to change things,
even small flowers stand in some relation to a cedar of Lebanon,
then he walked on and saw the windows of the furriers
were full of warm things for the winter ahead.


## III

All very well, a gin and a few minutes
in the park at noon, with the sun shining,
but what about when the landlord comes by, and there are problems
with your tax return, and the girlfriend's in tears?

Shattered: how far are you allowed to push your I,
and see a given detail as somehow symptomatic?
Shattered: to what extent are you obliged to play by the rules—
as far as a Ludwig Richter canvas?

Verzehrt: man weiß es nicht. Verzehrt: man wendet
sich qualvoll Einzel zu wie Allgemein –
das Zwischenspiel von Macht des Schicksals endet
glorios und ewig, aber ganz allein.

Verflucht die Evergreens! Die Platten dröhnen!
Schnaps, Sonne, Zedern – was verhelfen sie
dem Ich, den Traum, den Wirt und Gott versöhnen –
die Stimmen krächzen und die Worte höhnen –
verließ das Haus und schloß die Rêverie.

Shattered: no one knows. Shattered and you turn
equally pained to singular and universal—
your little experiment with destiny will end
gloriously and forever, but quite alone.

Damned evergreens! Vinyl whines!
Gin, sun, cedars—what use are they
to help the self reconcile landlord, God, and dream—
voices warble and words mock—
left the house and closed his reverie.

## MENSCHEN GETROFFEN

Ich habe Menschen getroffen, die,
wenn man sie nach ihrem Namen fragte,
schüchtern – als ob sie gar nicht beanspruchen könnten,
auch noch eine Benennung zu haben –
„Fräulein Christian" antworteten und dann:
„wie der Vorname", sie wollten einem die Erfassung erleichtern,
kein schwieriger Name wie „Popiol" oder „Babendererde" –
„wie der Vorname" – bitte, belasten Sie Ihr Erinnerungsvermögen
   nicht!

Ich habe Menschen getroffen, die
mit Eltern und vier Geschwistern in einer Stube
aufwuchsen, nachts, die Finger in den Ohren,
am Küchenherde lernten,
hochkamen, äußerlich schön und ladylike wie Gräfinnen –
und innerlich sanft und fleißig wie Nausikaa,
die reine Stirn der Engel trugen.

Ich habe mich oft gefragt und keine Antwort gefunden,
woher das Sanfte und das Gute kommt,
weiß es auch heute nicht und muß nun gehn.

## PEOPLE MET

I have met people who,
asked after their names,
shyly—as if they had no title
to an appellation all to themselves—
replied "Fräulein Christian" and added:
"like the first name," they wanted to make it easy for the other,
not a difficult name like "Popiol" or "Babendererde"—
"like the first name"—please, don't burden your memory
    overmuch!

I have met people who
grew up in a single room with their parents
and four brothers and sisters, and studied at night
with their fingers in their ears at the kitchen table,
and still grew up to be beautiful and self-possessed as duchesses—
and innerly gentle and hardworking as Nausicaa,
clear-browed as angels.

I have often asked myself and never found an answer
whence kindness and gentleness come,
I don't know it to this day, and now must go myself.

## EBERESCHEN

Ebereschen – noch nicht ganz rot
von jenem Farbton, wo sie sich entwickeln
zu Nachglut, Vogelbeere, Herbst und Tod.

Ebereschen – noch etwas fahl,
doch siehe schon zu einem Strauß gebunden
ankündigend halbtief die Abschiedsstunden:
vielleicht nie mehr, vielleicht dies letzte Mal.

Ebereschen – dies Jahr und Jahre immerzu
in fahlen Tönen erst und dann in roten
gefärbt, gefüllt, gereift, zu Gott geboten –
wo aber fülltest, färbtest, reiftest du –?

## ROWANS

Rowans—not yet fully rowan red
not yet in that tone they take on later
of ember, berry, October, and death.

Rowans—still a little green about the gills,
but see them bundled into a leggy bouquet,
making their sotto voce farewells:
maybe never again, chum, or just this once.

Rowans—this year and all the years,
first that queasy greenish pink and then rowan red,
colored up, plumped, ripened, and offered to God—
but where was it you plumped, colored, and ripened?—

## LETZTER FRÜHLING

Nimm die Forsythien tief in dich hinein
und wenn der Flieder kommt, vermisch auch diesen
mit deinem Blut und Glück und Elendsein,
dem dunklen Grund, auf den du angewiesen.

Langsame Tage. Alles überwunden.
Und fragst du nicht, ob Ende, ob Beginn,
dann tragen dich vielleicht die Stunden
noch bis zum Juni mit den Rosen hin.

## LAST SPRING

Fill yourself up with the forsythias
and when the lilacs flower, stir them in too
with your blood and happiness and wretchedness,
the dark ground that seems to come with you.

Sluggish days. All obstacles overcome.
And if you say, ending or beginning, who knows,
then maybe—just maybe—the hours will carry you
into June, when roses blow.

# SPÄT

I

Die alten schweren Bäume
in großen Parks
und die Blumengärten,
die feucht verwirrten –

herbstliche Süße,
Polster von Erika
die Autobahn entlang,
alles ist Lüneburger
Heide, lila und unfruchtbar,
Versonnenheiten, die zu Nichts führen,
in sich gekehrtes Kraut,
das bald hinabbräunt
– Frage eines Monats –
ins Nieerblühte.

Dies die Natur.
Und durch die City
in freundlichem Licht
fahren die Bierwagen
Ausklangssänfte, auch Unbesorgnis

# LATE

I

The big old trees
in the parks,
and the flower beds
all damp and tangled—

autumnal sweetness,
tuffets of erica
along the Autobahn,
everything is Lüneburg
heather, purple and unbearing,
whins going nowhere,
introverted stuff
soon browned off—
give it a month
it'll be as if it'd never flowered.

So much for nature.
And through the city
in the blinking light
beer trucks deliver tranquillity,
unconcern with thirst and desires—

vor Reizzuständen, Durst und Ungestilltem —
was stillt sich nicht? Nur kleine Kreise!
Die großen schwelgen
in Übermaßen.


II


So enden die Blicke, die Blicke zurück:
Felder und Seen eingewaschen in deine Tage
und die ersten Lieder
aus einem alten Klavier.

Begegnungen der Seele! Jugend!
Dann selbst gestaltet
Treubruch, Verfehlen, Verfall —
die Hintergründe der Glücke.

Und Liebe!
„Ich glaube dir, daß du gerne bei mir geblieben wärest,
aber es nicht konntest,
ich spreche dich frei von jeder Schuld“ —
ja, Liebe
schwer und vielgestalt,
jahrelang verborgen
werden wir einander zurufen: „nicht vergessen“,
bis einer tot ist — —
so enden die Rosen,
Blatt um Blatt.

what is it doesn't quench itself?
Only small circles!
The big ones wallow
in excess.


II


Memory comes down to this:
fields and lakes fused with your days,
early tunes
on an old piano.

Shy souls! Youth!
Then, seemingly all by themselves,
infidelity, lapse, slip from grace—
the backgrounds to bliss.

And love.
"I do believe you really wanted to stay with me,
but weren't able to.
I don't blame you for what happened,"
yes, love,
heavy and variegated,
after keeping our secret for years
we will call out to one another: "don't forget,"
till one of us is dead—
so the roses go,
petal by petal.

III

Noch einmal so sein wie früher:
unverantwortlich und nicht das Ende wissen,
das Fleisch fühlen: Durst, Zärtlichkeit, Erobern, Verlieren,
hinüberlangen in jenes Andere – in was?

Abends dasitzen, in den Schlund der Nacht sehn,
er verengert sich, aber am Grund sind Blumen,
es duftet herauf, kurz und zitternd,
dahinter natürlich die Verwesung,
dann ist es ganz dunkel und du weißt wieder dein Teil,
wirfst dein Geld hin und gehst –

soviel Lügen geliebt,
soviel Worten geglaubt,
die nur aus der Wölbung der Lippen kamen,
und dein eigenes Herz
so wandelbar, bodenlos und augenblicklich –

soviel Lügen geliebt,
soviel Lippen gesucht
(„nimm das Rouge von deinem Munde,
gib ihn mir blaß")

und der Fragen immer mehr –

III

To be as one once was:
irresponsible, no knowledge of how things end,
be guided by the flesh: thirst, tenderness, conquest, loss,
the reaching across into the other—whomever or whatever.

To sit there of an evening, staring down night's throat,
a narrowing funnel, but at the bottom are flowers,
scent climbs, trembly and brief,
followed of course by putrefaction,
then it's completely dark, and you remember what you came for,
and put down your money and leave—

loved so many lies,
believed so many words
spoken by curved lips
and your own heart
so impulsive, bottomless, changeable—

loved so many lies,
sought so many lips
("oh, wipe the lipstick off your mouth,
give it me pale")

and ever more questions—

Little old lady
in a big red room
little old lady –
summt Marion Davies,
während Hearst, ihr Freund seit 30 Jahren,
in schwerem Kupfersarg unter dem Schutz einer starken Eskorte
und gefolgt von 22 Limousinen
vor dem Marmormausoleum eintrifft,
leise surren die Fernkameras.

Little old lady, großer roter Raum,
hennarot, sanft gladiolenrot, kaiserrot (Purpurschnecke),
Schlafzimmer in Santa Monica Schloß
à la Pompadour –

Louella, ruft sie, Radio!
Die Blues, Jitterbug – Zickzack!
Das Bürgertum im atlantischen Raum:
heiratsfähige Töchter und obliterierter Sexus,
Palazzos an den Bays, Daunendecken auf den Pfühlen,
die Welt teilen sie ein in Monde und Demimonde –
ich war immer letzteres –

Louella, meine Mischung – hochprozentig!
Was soll das alles –
gedemütigt, hochgekämpft, hündisch gelitten –
die Züge, häßliche Züge, mit denen jetzt der Kupfersarg Schluß
    macht,

IV

Little old lady
in a big red room
little old lady—
hums Marion Davies
while Hearst, her lover of 30 years,
arrives outside the marble mausoleum
with the protection of a numerous escort
and followed by 22 limousines, lying in a heavy copper coffin
all to the quiet whine of the TV cameras.

Little old lady, big red room,
henna red, plush gladioli red, Tyrian purple (that wee snail
    in the Med),
the bedroom in the Castle in Santa Monica
done up à la Pompadour—

Louella, she calls, radio!
The blues, jitterbug—zigzag!
Upper classes up and down the Atlantic,
marriageable daughters, obliterated urges,
palazzos on the water, down comforters on the mattresses,
the world was divided between rep and demi-rep—
I was always the latter—

Louella, my tincture!
What's it all for—
Humiliation, revival, more, atrocious suffering—
his features, ugly features, now sealed in the copper coffin,

überrann ein Licht, wenn er mich sah,
auch Reiche lieben, zittern, kennen die Verdammnis.

Hochprozentig – das Glas an den Silberapparat,
er wird nun stumm sein zu jener Stunde,
die nur wir beide wußten –
drollige Sprüche kamen aus der Muschel,
„in Frühstücksstuben entscheidet sich das Leben,
am Strand im Bathdreß hagelt es Granit,
das Unerwartete pflegt einzutreten,
das Erhoffte geschieht nie –"
das waren seine Stories.

Schluß mit der Promenade! Nur noch einige Steinfliesen,
auf die vorderste das Glas,
hochprozentig, Klirren, letzte Rhapsodie –
little old lady,
in a big red room –


V


Fühle – doch wisse, Jahrtausende fühlten –
Meer und Getier und die kopflosen Sterne
ringen es nieder heute wie einst –

denke – doch wisse, die Allererlauchtesten
treiben in ihrem eigenen Kiel,
sind nur das Gelb der Butterblume,
auch andere Farben spielen ihr Spiel –

he would crash the lights when he saw me,
even a wealthy man can love and tremble and feel hellfire.

Neat—the glass by the silver shaker,
he's silent now, though it's our hour of the day
our private time—
strange things he would say on the phone,
"life gets settled over the breakfast table,"
"hailstones feel like granite if you're on the beach in swimming
     costume,"
"the unexpected always happens,
the hoped-for never does—"
those were his moralities.

Constitutional over. Just a few more flagstones,
set the glass down on the last,
neat, plink of ice, last rhapsody,
little old lady,
big red room—


          V


Feel it—but remember, millennia have felt it—
the sea and the beasts and the mindless stars
wrestle it down today as ever—

think it—but remember, the most exalted
are wallowing in their own bow wave,
are no more than the yellow of the buttercup,
while other colors too play their game—

wisse das alles und trage die Stunde,
keine wie diese, jede wie sie,
Menschen und Engel und Cherubime,
Schwarzgeflügeltes, Hellgeäugtes,
keines war deines –
deines nie.


VI


Siehst du es nicht, wie einige halten,
viele wenden den Rücken zu,
seltsame hohe schmale Gestalten,
alle wandern den Brücken zu.

Senken die Stecken, halten die Uhren
an, die Ziffern brauchen kein Licht,
schwindende Scharen, schwarze Figuren,
alle weinen – siehst du es nicht?

remember and endure the hour,
there was never one like it / all are like it,
people and angels and cherubim,
black-winged, bright-eyed,
none was yours—
was ever yours.


V I


Do you not see how a few stop,
and many turn their backs,
strange lean shapes,
all making for the bridges.

Lower their sticks, stop the clock,
the clockface needs no light,
vanishing hordes, black shapes,
all weeping, do you not see?

## ZERSTÖRUNGEN

Zerstörungen –
aber wo nichts mehr zu zerstören ist,
selbst die Trümmer altern
mit Wegerich und Zichorie
auf ihren Humusandeutungen,
verkrampft als Erde –

Zerstörungen –
das sagt immerhin: hier war einmal
Masse, Gebautes, Festgefügtes –
o schönes Wort
voll Anklang
an Füllungsreichtum
und Heimatfluren –

Zerstörungen –
o graues Siebenschläferwort
mit Wolken, Schauern, Laubverdunkeltheiten,
gesichert für lange Zeit –
wo Sommer sein sollte
mit Fruchtgetränken,
Eisbechern, beschlagenen,
und Partys zu heller Nacht am Strande.

## DEVASTATIONS

Devastations—
but where there's nothing more to devastate,
even the ruins are mellowing,
chicory and plantain sprouting
from tumps of rubble
smooshed to humus—

devastations—
still proclaim: here were once
mass, construction, foundations—
proud word
evocative of
plenitude
and acres of home—

devastations—
gray Rip Van Winkle word
with clouds, showers, gloomy leafshadow,
and all of long duration—
where summer should have been,
with fruit punch,
dishes of ice cream beaded on the outside,
and beach parties in the white nights.

## DAS SIND DOCH MENSCHEN

Das sind doch Menschen, denkt man,
wenn der Kellner an einen Tisch tritt,
einen unsichtbaren,
Stammtisch oder dergleichen in einer Ecke,
das sind doch Zartfühlende, Genüßlinge
sicher auch mit Empfindungen und Leid.

So allein bist du nicht
in deinem Wirrwar, Unruhe, Zittern,
auch da wird Zweifel sein, Zaudern, Unsicherheit,
wenn auch in Geschäftsabschlüssen,
das Allgemein-Menschliche,
zwar in Wirtschaftsformen,
auch dort!

Unendlich ist der Gram der Herzen
und allgemein,
aber ob sie je geliebt haben
(außerhalb des Bettes)
brennend, verzehrt, wüstendurstig
nach einem Gaumenpfirsichsaft
aus fernem Mund,
untergehend, ertrinkend
in Unvereinbarkeit der Seelen –

## THEY ARE HUMAN AFTER ALL

They are human after all, you think,
as the waiter steps up to a table
out of sight of you,
reserved, corner table,
they too are thin-skinned and pleasure-seeking,
with their own feelings and their own sufferings.

You're not so all alone
in your mess, your restlessness, your shakes,
they too will be full of doubt, dither, shilly-shallying,
even if it's all about making deals,
the universal human
albeit in its commercial manifestation,
but present there too.

Truly, the grief of hearts is ubiquitous
and unending,
but whether they were ever in love
(outwith the awful wedded bed)
burning, athirst, desert-parched
for the nectar of a faraway
mouth,
sinking, drowning
in the impossibility of a union of souls—

das weiß man nicht, kann auch
den Kellner nicht fragen,
der an der Registrierkasse
das neue Helle eindrückt,
des Bons begierig,
um einen Durst zu löschen anderer Art,
doch auch von tiefer.

you won't know, nor can you
ask the waiter,
who's just ringing up
another Beck's,
always avid for coupons
to quench a thirst of another nature,
though also deep.

## TEILS-TEILS

In meinem Elternhaus hingen keine Gainsboroughs
wurde auch kein Chopin gespielt
ganz amusisches Gedankenleben
mein Vater war einmal im Theater gewesen
Anfang des Jahrhunderts
Wildenbruchs „Haubenlerche"
davon zehrten wir
das war alles.

Nun längst zu Ende
graue Herzen, graue Haare
der Garten in polnischem Besitz
die Gräber teils-teils
aber alle slawisch,
Oder-Neiße-Linie
für Sarginhalte ohne Belang
die Kinder denken an sie
die Gatten auch noch eine Weile
teils-teils
bis sie weitermüssen
Sela, Psalmenende.

Heute noch in einer Großstadtnacht
Caféterrasse

## PAR CI, PAR LÀ

There were no Gainsboroughs in my parents' house
and no one played Chopin
perfectly philistrous intellectual life
my father had been to the theater once
in the early century
Wildenbruch's *Crested Lark*
that was our pabulum
there was nothing else.

All long gone now
gray hearts, gray hair
the garden in Polish hands
the graves *par ci, par là*
but all on the Slavic side
Oder-Neisse Line
inapplicable to the contents of coffins
the children continue to think about them
the spouses too for a while
*par ci, par là*
till it's time for them to move on
Selah, end of psalm.

Even now in the big city night
café terrace

Sommersterne,
vom Nebentisch
Hotelqualitäten in Frankfurt
Vergleiche,
die Damen unbefriedigt
wenn ihre Sehnsucht Gewicht hätte
wöge jede drei Zentner.

Aber ein Fluidum! Heiße Nacht
à la Reiseprospekt und
die Ladies treten aus ihren Bildern:
unwahrscheinliche Beauties
langbeinig, hoher Wasserfall
über ihre Hingabe kann man sich gar nicht erlauben
nachzudenken.

Ehepaare fallen demgegenüber ab,
kommen nicht an, Bälle gehn ins Netz,
er raucht, sie dreht ihre Ringe,
überhaupt nachdenkenswert
Verhältnis von Ehe und Mannesschaffen
Lähmung oder Hochtrieb.

Fragen, Fragen! Erinnerungen in einer Sommernacht
hingeblinzelt, hingestrichen,
in meinem Elternhaus hingen keine Gainsboroughs
nun alles abgesunken
teils-teils das Ganze
Sela, Psalmenende.

summer stars
from the next-door table
assessments
of hotels in Frankfurt
the ladies frustrated
if their desires had mass
they would each of them weigh twenty stone.

But the electricity in the air! Balmy night
à la travel brochure and
the girls step out of their pictures
improbable lovelies
legs up to here, a waterfall,
their surrender is something one daren't even begin
to contemplate.

Married couples by comparison disappoint,
don't cut it, fail to clear the net,
he smokes, she twists her rings,
worth considering
the whole relationship between marriage and creativity,
stifling or galvanizing.

Questions, questions! Scribbled nictitations
on a summer night,
there were no Gainsboroughs in my parents' house
now everything has gone under
the whole thing, *par ci, par là*,
Selah, end of psalm.

## KEINER WEINE –

Rosen, gottweißwoher so schön,
in grünen Himmeln die Stadt
abends
in der Vergänglichkeit der Jahre!

Mit welcher Sehnsucht gedenke ich der Zeit,
wo mir eine Mark dreißig lebenswichtig waren,
ja, notgedrungen, ich sie zählte,
meine Tage ihnen anpassen mußte,
was sage ich Tage: Wochen, mit Brot und Pflaumenmus
aus irdenen Töpfen
vom heimatlichen Dorf mitgenommen,
noch von häuslicher Armut beschienen,
wie weh war alles, wie schön und zitternd!

Was soll der Glanz der europäischen Auguren,
der großen Namen,
der Pour le mérite,
die auf sich sehn und weiter schaffen,

ach, nur Vergehendes ist schön,
rückblickend die Armut,
sowie das Dumpfe, das sich nicht erkennt,
schluchzt und stempeln geht,

## NO TEARS

Roses, Christ knows how they got to be so lovely,
green skies over the city
in the evening
in the ephemerality of the years!

The yearning I have for that time
when one mark thirty was all I had,
yes, I counted them this way and that,
I trimmed my days to fit them,
days, what am I saying days: weeks on bread and plum mush
out of earthenware pots
brought from my village,
still under the rushlight of native poverty,
how raw everything felt, how tremblingly beautiful!

What good is the luster conferred by European pundits,
the great names,
the *Pour le Mérite*s,
people who shoot their cuffs and tool on,

it's only the ephemeral that's beautiful,
looking back, the poverty,
the frowstiness that didn't know what it was,
sobs, and stands in line for its dole,

wunderbar dieser Hades,
der das Dumpfe nimmt
wie die Auguren –

keiner weine,
keiner sage: ich, so allein.

what a wonderful Hades
that takes away the frowst,
and the pundits both—

please, no tears,
no one say: oh, I was so lonesome.

FROM UNCOLLECTED AND
POSTHUMOUS POEMS

# EXPRESSIONIST!

Eine Münze wird man dir nicht prägen,
wie es Griechenland für Sappho tat,
daß man dir nicht einschlägt deinen Brägen,
ist in Deutschland schon Kultur-verrat.

# EXPRESSIONIST!

They won't stamp a medal with your mug shot
the way the Greeks did for Sappho;
if they failed to beat your brains out, that already
is accounted actionable and treason, in Germany.

## 1886

Ostern am spätesten Termin,
an der Elbe blühte schon der Flieder,
dafür Anfang Dezember ein so unerhörter Schneefall,
daß der gesamte Bahnverkehr
in Nord- und Mitteldeutschland
für Wochen zum Erliegen kam.

Paul Heyse veröffentlicht eine einaktige Tragödie,
Es ist Hochzeitsabend, die junge Frau entdeckt,
daß ihr Mann einmal ihre Mutter geliebt hat,
alle längst tot, immerhin
von ihrer Tante, die Mutterstelle vertrat,
hat sie ein Morphiumfläschchen:
„störe das sanfte Mittel nicht",
sie sinkt zurück, hascht nach seiner Hand,
Theodor (düster, aufschreiend):
„Lydia! Mein Weib! Nimm mich mit Dir"! –
Titel: „Zwischen Lipp' und Kelchesrand".

England erobert Mandelai,
eröffnet das weite Tal des Irawaday dem Welthandel;
Madagaskar kommt an Frankreich;
Rußland vertreibt den Fürsten Alexander
aus Bulgarien.

## 1886

Easter that year at the latest possible date,
the lilac was already in flower along the Elbe,
but to make up for it such a heavy snowfall in the first week of
    December
that the entire rail network
of Northern and Central Germany
was paralyzed for weeks.

Paul Heyse publishes a one-act tragedy,
young bride on the eve of her wedding discovers
that the groom once loved her mother,
now long since dead, but
from her aunt, who raised her,
she still has a phial of morphine:
"do not disturb the gentle agent,"
she sinks back, reaching for his hand,
Theodor (frantic, shouting):
"Lydia! My wife! Take me with you!"—
Title: "'Twixt Cup and Lip."

The British conquer Mandalay,
open up the wide valley of the Irrawaddy to world trade;
France acquires Madagascar;
the Russians expel Count Alexander
from Bulgaria.

Der Deutsche Radfahrbund
zählt 1500 Mitglieder.
Güßfeldt besteigt zum ersten Mal
den Montblanc
über den Grand Mulet.
Die Barsois aus dem Perchinozwinger
im Gouvernement Tula,
die mit der besonders tiefbefahnten Brust,
die Wolfsjäger,
erscheinen auf der Berliner Hundeausstellung,
Asmodey erhält die Goldene Medaille.

Die Registertonne wird einheitlich
auf 2,8 cbm Raumgehalt festgesetzt;
Übergang des Raddampfers zum Schraubendampfer;
Rückgang der Holzschiffe;
über das chinesische Kauffahrteiwesen
ist statistisch nichts bekannt;
Norddeutscher Lloyd: 38 Schiffe, 63 000 t,
Hamburg – Amerika: 19 Schiffe, 34 200 t,
Hamburg-Süd: 9 Schiffe, 13 500 t.

Turgenjew in Baden-Baden
besucht täglich die Schwestern Viardot,
unvergeßliche Abende,
sein Lieblingslied, das selten gehörte:
„wenn meine Grillen schwirren"
(Schubert),
oft auch lesen sie Scheffel's Ekkehard.

The Association of German Cyclists
has 1,500 members.
Güßfeldt becomes the first man to scale
Mont Blanc
via the Grand Mulet.
Borzois from the Perkhino kennels
in the province of Tula,
the ones with the particularly deep blazons on their chest,
used in the hunting of wolves,
are favorites for the Berlin equivalent of Crufts,
the Gold Medal is awarded to one Asmodey.

The shipping ton is fixed
at 2.8 cubic meters;
transition from paddle wheel to screw propeller;
last days of wooden clippers;
no statistics available
on the Chinese merchantman fleet;
North German Lloyd: 38 vessels, 63,000 tons,
Hamburg America Line: 19 vessels, 34,200 tons,
Hamburg-Süd: 9 vessels, 13,500 tons.

In Baden-Baden Turgenev
pays daily visits to the Viardot sisters,
unforgettable evenings,
his favorite lied
Schubert's rarely heard
"wenn meine Grillen schwirren,"
or they just read aloud from Scheffel's *Ekkehard*.

Es werden entdeckt:
der flügellose Vogel Kiwi-kiwi in Neuseeland,
der augenlose Molch in der Krainer Tropfsteinklamm,
ein blinder Fisch in der Mammuthhöhle von Kentucky.
Beobachtet werden:
Schwinden des Haarkleides (Wale, Delphine),
Weißlichwerden der Haut (Schnecken, Köcherfliegen),
Panzerrückbildung (Krebse, Insekten) –
Entwicklungsfragen,
Befruchtungsstudien,
Naturgeheimnis,
nachgestammelt.

Kampf gegen Fremdwörter,
Luna, Cephir, Chrysalide,
1088 Wörter aus dem Faust
sollen verdeutscht werden.
Agitation der Handlungsgehilfen
für Schließung der Geschäfte an den Sonntagnachmittagen,
sozialdemokratische Stimmen
bei der Wahl in Berlin: 68 535.
Das Tiergartenviertel ist freisinnig,
Singer hält seine erste
Kandidatenrede.
13. Auflage von Brockhaus'
Konversationslexikon.

Die Zeitungen beklagen die Aufführung
von Tolstoi's „Macht der Finsternis",

The following are discovered:
the flightless kiwi-kiwi bird in New Zealand,
the eyeless newt in the limestone caverns at Kranj,
a blind fish in the Mammoth Caves of Kentucky.
The following are investigated:
the erosion of hair covering (whales, dolphins),
the whitening of skin (snails, caddis flies),
formation of body armor (crabs, insects)—
questions of evolution,
fertility studies,
nature's secrets
lisped back.

Campaign against foreign words,
luna moth, zephyr, chrysalis,
1,088 dictionary terms
are to be Germanized.
Shop assistants strike for Sunday afternoons off,
the number of votes polled
by the Social Democrats
in the Berlin election: 68,535.
The Tiergarten ward is free thinking.
Singer gives his first speech
as a candidate.
13th edition of the *Brockhaus*
encyclopedia.

The critics savage Tolstoy's
*Power of Darkness,*

dagegen ist Blumenthal's „Ein Tropfen Gift"
eines langen Nachklangs von Wohllaut sicher;
„Über dem Haupt des Grafen Albrecht Vahlberg,
der eine geachtete Stellung in der hauptstädtischen Gesellschaft
einnimmt,
schwebt eine dunkle Wolke",
Zola, Ibsen, Hauptmann sind unerfreulich,
Salambo verfehlt,
Liszt Kosmopolit,
und nun kommt die Rubrik
„Der Leser hat das Wort",
er will etwas wissen
über Wadenkrämpfe
und Fremdkörperentfernung.

Es taucht auf:
Pithekanthropos,
Javarudimente, –
die Vorstufen.
Es stirbt aus:
der kleine Vogel von Hawai
für die königlichen Federmäntel:
ein gelber Flaumstreif an jedem Flügel, –
genannt der Honigsauger.

1886 –
Geburtsjahr gewisser Expressionisten,
ferner von Staatsrat Furtwängler,

while Blumenthal's *A Drop of Poison*
is guaranteed a long euphuous run;
"A dark cloud hangs
over the head of Count Albrecht Vahlberg,
who occupies a respected place in society in the capital,"
Zola, Ibsen, Hauptmann
are unwelcome,
*Salammbô* misconceived,
Liszt cosmopolitan,
and last but not least comes the slot
"The reader writes,"
the explanation of cramp
and the removal of foreign bodies
are what he wants explained to him.

First appearances of:
*Pithecanthropus,*
Java remnants,
the avatars.
Rendered extinct:
the little Hawaiian fellow
called the sunbird
used in the making of feather coats for the royal family,
a yellow streak of fluff on each wing,

1886—
birth year of certain expressionists,
also of state councillor Furtwängler,

Emigrant Kokoschka,
Generalfeldmarschall v. W. (†),

Kapitalverdoppelung
bei Schneider-Creusot, Krupp-Stahl, Putiloff.

emigré Kokoschka,
General Field Marshall von W— (†),

doubling of equity
at Schneider-Creusot, Putilov, Krupp Steel.

## STILLE

Stille,
belebt von Innen her:
Gewesenheiten
ganz frühe Bande,
zarte, todgelöste;
auch Tage voll von Büschen von Jasmin
und Früchteschalen zwischen einem Paar
fragloser Gläubigkeit, zwei Flammen.

Stille,
von fernen Höfen her
Bereitungen von Fest und Heimatfühlen:
Klopfen von Teppichen,
auf denen, frisch gerichtet,
dann Schritte vieler gehn
in Glück und Liebe.

Stille,
das Einstige und Kommendes für Fremde,
und wo das Heutige, ein dunkler Laut:
„bleib noch an meiner Seite,
vielleicht nicht lange mehr,
zuviel Verfall in mir
zu schwer
und müde.“

## SILENCE

Silence,
coming from within:
things past,
tender early associations
ended by death;
also days with table decorations and fruit bowls
placed between couples
of unwavering commitment, two flames.

Silence,
from faraway estates,
preparations for festivities or homecomings:
beating of carpets,
on which, later,
many pairs of feet will shuffle
in love and dotage.

Silence,
once offered to and endured by strangers,
broken today by a gruff plea:
"stay by me,
maybe not all that much longer,
so much decay in me,
so much heaviness,
fatigue."

## NASSE ZÄUNE

Nasse Zäune
über Land geweht,
dunkelgrüne Stakete,
Krähenunruhe und Pappelentblätterung
als Umwelt.

Nasse Zäune,
Gartenabgrenzung,
doch nicht für Abkömmlinge
der berühmten Tulpe Semper Augustus,
die Paris im 17. Jahrhundert mit unerhörten Preisen
bezahlte,
oder die Hyazinthe „Bleu Passe"
(1600 fl. anno 1734),
man trug seinen Namen in ein Buch ein,
erst mehrere Tage später
führte einen ein Gartendirektor vorbei −,
vielmehr für die alten bewährten Ranunkeln Ostades.

Nasse Zäune,
Holzfäulnis und Moosansatz
in der Stille der Dörfer,

## WET FENCES

Wet fences
blown over the land,
dark green stakes,
murders of crows and shedding poplars
for company.

Wet fences
defining gardens,
though not for descendants
of the renowned tulip Semper Augustus
which in 17th-century Paris
changed hands for unheard-of sums,
or the hyacinth "Bleu Passe"
(1600, floruit 1734),
for which you wrote down your name in a book,
and several days later
a head gardener would conduct you past it—
rather for the old and reliable ranunculi of Ostade.

Wet fences,
moldering and putting on moss
in the silent villages,

kleine Ordnungszeile
über Land geweht,
doch Schnee und Salze sammeln sich,
rinnen Verfall –
die alten Laute.

little barriers
blown over the land,
but snow collects, and corrosive salts,
dribble of rot—
the old story.

## CLÉMENCEAU

„Mit dem Blick auf das Ende
ist das Leben schön“,
der Blick lag auf den Rosen der Vendée.
Ferner:
„die Menschen haben keine Seele,
wenn sie doch wenigstens Haltung hätten.“

Ein überlegenes Gefühl zeigt folgende Bemerkung:
„es gibt Sterne,
die seit 2000 Jahren erloschen sind
und deren Licht wir noch erhalten.
Wenn man daran denkt,
ist alles in Ordnung.“

Über Kunst wußte er Bescheid.
Betreffend seinen Gutsnachbar Monet schrieb er:
„er hätte noch zehn Jahre leben müssen,
dann hätte man nichts von dem verstanden,
was er schuf,
auf seiner Leinewand
wäre dann vielleicht nichts mehr zu sehn gewesen.“

Witzig ist folgender Dialog:
„C.: er soll ein leidenschaftlicher Päderast
gewesen sein?

## CLÉMENCEAU

"With one eye on the end,
life is beautiful,"
the eye was on the roses of the Vendée.
Moreover,
"Human beings have no souls,
if only they had a bit of dignity."

A superior feeling is indicated by the following remark:
"There are stars
that have been extinguished for 2,000 years,
and we still see their light.
If you bear that in mind,
everything's okay."

He knew about art.
On his country neighbor Monet he wrote:
"If he'd been given another ten years to live,
no one would have understood the least bit
of his work,
maybe his canvases would have had
nothing on them at all."

The following dialogue is amusing:
"C: So, he is said to have been
an enthusiastic pederast?

M.: nein, er spricht von Päderastie,
ohne sich zu erregen.
C.: was, er erregte sich nicht einmal?"

Hinsichtlich unserer Besonderheit scherzte er:
„die Deutschen sehen,
wie ein niedliches Tier im Waser umhertändelt
und das nennen sie dann Meerschwein."

Die Perspektive tritt an Stelle der Emphase;
fünfundachtzigjährig faßte er zusammen:
„nichts ist wahr. Alles ist wahr.
Das ist der Weisheit letzter Schluß."

Oft war er in Griechenland gewesen,
hatte von der Akropolis Manches mitgebracht;
sein Testament schloß:
„auf mein Grab den Marmor aus Hellas."

M: No, he talks about it,
without getting at all excited.
C: What, he didn't even get excited?"

On the subject of our little faible he jested:
"The Germans
see an adorable beast sashaying into the water
and then they call it a sea-pig."*

In place of emphasis, perspective;
aged eighty-five, he offered the following summing-up:
"Nothing is true. Everything is true.
That's the end of wisdom."

He had been many times to Greece,
had brought home pieces from the Acropolis;
his will ended:
"On my tomb the marble from Hellas."

* *"Meerschweinchen"* ("little sea-pig") is the German term for "guinea pig."

# KLEINES SÜSSES GESICHT

Kleines süßes Gesicht,
eingesunken schon vor Vergängnis,
schneeblaß und tötlich,
Ausschütter großen Leids,
wenn du hingegangen
bald —

ach, wie wir spielten
entwicklungsvergessen,
Rück- und Weitblicke
abgefallen von unseren Rändern,
nichts lebend
außer dem Umkreis
unserer Laute!

Beschränkt! Doch dann
einmal der astverborgenen Männer
Oliven Niederschlagen,
die Haufen gären.
Einmal Weine vom Löwengolf
in Rauchkammern, mit Seewasser beschönigt.
Oder Eukalyptus, Riesen, 156 Meter hoch
und das zitternde Zwielicht in ihren Wäldern.
Einmal Cotroceni —
nicht mehr!

## LITTLE SWEET FACE

Little sweet face,
shrunken already in transit,
snowy-, nearly deathly pale,
great outpouring of grief
when you shortly passed
away—

We played together
quite unmindful of our state of development
all looks back and out
cropped,
living, experiencing nothing
outside the charmed circle
of our own noises!

Hobbled—blinkered! But once,
the men beating the olive trees, obscured by branches,
piles of fruit set to ripen.
Once, wine from the Gulf of Lions
in smoky vaults, accented with seawater.
Or giant eucalypts, 400 feet high,
and the trembling light under their crowns.
Once to Cotroceni—
once only.

Kleines Gesicht
Schneeflocke
immer so weiß
und dann die Ader an der Schläfe
vom Blau der Traubenhyazinthe,
die ligurische,
die bisamartig duftet.

Little face
snowflake
always so white
and the blue vein at the temple
Ligurian grape hyacinth
blue,
musk-scented.

Wie sehn die Buchen im September aus
am Oeresund, dem Gardasee des Nordens,
an dem soviel Rittersporn blüht
wie sonst in ganz Europa nicht zusammen
und drüben Sverige,
das stolze Land.

Armer German sitzt am Wasser
fragt er etwas auf Deutsch
spucken ihn die Leute an,
fragt er französisch,
verstehn es die Leute nicht
u dänisch ist eine schwere Sprache
weich u süß wie Schlagsahne

Alter German,
lange auf Galeere gerudert,
wer auf Galeere sitzt
sieht die Wasser von unten
kann die Ufer nicht beobachten
die Möven nicht verfolgen
alles Schiffsbauch
Schimmelzwieback
Fußfessel,
Schlick Impressionen
für hohes Leben

How are the beech trees in September
on the Øresund, the Garda of the North,
where as much larkspur flowers
as in the whole of the rest of Europe,
and yonder Sverige,
the proud country.

Poor German sits by the water's edge
if he asks a question in German
the people spit at him,
if he asks it in French
the people don't understand,
and Danish is a difficult language
sweet & soft as whipped cream

Old German
a long time rowing in the galleys,
who-sits-in-galley-
will-see-water-from-below,
incapable of watching the shore
or following the seagulls
all ship's belly
moldy zwieback
leg irons,
oil-slick impressions
of the higher life.

## DIVERGENZEN

Der Eine sagt: nur kein Innenleben
Höflichkeit, aber kein Gemüt,
das kompensiert nicht mehr
die unerträglichen, extrovertierten
Ausdrucksspannungen –
der cerebralisierten
City-Styxe

wenn mein Bub, das Strampelchen
sein Beinchen aus dem Bett streckt,
bin ich geliefert, das war bei Otto Ernst so
u ist es noch heute

Schwer vereinbare Gegensätze,
wenn man die Provinzen überblickt,
hat das Innenleben
das Übergewicht.

## DIVERGENCES

One says: please no inner life,
manners are all right but nothing affective,
that's no compensation
for the insufferable
difficulties of outward-directed expression—
those cerebralized
city Styxes

when my little prince
pokes his chubby little legs through the bars of his cot
it melts my heart, it was like that with Otto Ernst,
& it's no different now

the contraries are hard to reconcile
when you survey the provinces
the inner life
has it by a neck.

## HERR WEHNER

Dies ist meiner
dieser Herr Wehner
der bei uns Hauslehrer war
früh an Lungenphtise verschied
nachdem er meinen jüngsten Bruder angesteckt hatte,
der starb an meningitis tuberkulosa.

Stammte aus Lissa
Sohne eines Schmiedes
ging immer in Holzpantinen
was bei uns unüblich war,
seine Braut Liska
war einen Pfingsten bei uns
Tochter eines Polizeimajors
also was Besseres
sie kicherten oft abends
wenn die Mücken summten
und wir schlafen gehn mußten
aber, wie ich später hörte,
war es wohl doch nichts Rechtes.

Dieser Herr Wehner
ist insofern meiner

## HERR WEHNER

This is mine
Herr Wehner
he was our house tutor
died early of phthisis
once he'd infected my youngest brother
who died of tubercular meningitis.

Came from Lissa
son of a blacksmith
always went around in wooden clogs
which was unusual with us
Liska, his bride,
stayed with us over Whitsun once
daughter of a police major
ergo different class
the giggling in the evenings
when the mosquitoes buzzed
and it was our bedtime,
but, as I heard later,
it was a rocky marriage.

Herr Wehner,
what makes him mine

als er irgendwo begraben liegt,
vermodert in polnischem Kombinat,
keiner der Gemeindemitglieder
wird seiner gedenken,
aber vor mit steigt er manchmal auf
grau und isoliert
unter geschichtlichen Aspekten.

is the fact that he is buried somewhere
rotting away in a collective farm in (now) Poland
no one in the village
will remember him
but he sometimes appears to me
gray and isolated
under certain historical aspects.

## KLEINER KULTURSPIEGEL

Die Zeitalter wechseln langsam,
Tosca (1902) ist immer noch die Leidenschaft,
Bohème (1900) die Liebe,
selbst aus dem Schluß der Götterdämmerung (1876)
stürzen immer noch unsere Scheite.
Einiges blieb schemenhaft:
Iphigenie, V. Akt
(bei der Premiere 1779 spielte Goethe den Orest):
Thoas's Verzicht und Humanitas
hat sich politisch
nicht durchgesetzt.

Die Iden des März stehn in Zwielicht:
wenn eine neue Regierungsform hochwill,
muß die alte weichen.
Über Leonidas wird heute die Mehrzahl lachen
(ich persönlich allerdings nicht).

Ein Frisör, der wirklich gut rasiert,
(äußerst selten!)
ist bemerkenswerter als ein Hofprediger
(ich verkenne das Tragische und das Schuldproblem nicht).

## LITTLE CULTURAL COMMENTARY

Epochs change slowly,
*Tosca* (1902) is still passion,
*Bohème* (1900) is love,
even from the end of *Twilight of the Gods* (1876)
it's still our ashes that glow.
Some things remain sketchy:
*Iphigenia* Act V
(at the premiere in 1779, Goethe himself played Orestes):
Thoas's renunciation and humanity
never established themselves
in the political repertoire.

The Ides of March stand in twilight:
if a new form of government is coming,
the old one must make way.
Most people laugh at Leonidas today
(I myself don't).

A barber who delivers a first-class shave
(extremely rare!)
is more remarkable than a court chaplain
(I don't mistake tragedy and the problem of guilt).

Und sprechen Sie viel von der Lebensangst
zum Frühstück etwas Midgardschlange,
abends Okeanos, das Unbegrenzte,
nachts die Geworfenheit – dann schläft es sich gut ein –
Verteidigen will sich das Abendland nicht mehr –
Angst will es haben, geworfen will es sein.

Ein Schlager von Rang ist mehr 1950
als 500 Seiten Kulturkrise.
Im Kino, wo man Hut und Mantel mitnehmen kann,
ist mehr Feuerwasser als auf dem Kothurn
und ohne die lästige Pause.

(Das Quartär war der nach Innen gewendete Mensch,
jetzt kommt der triploide)
66 Chromosomen, Riesenwuchs –,

Und nun die neue Nationalhymne!
Der Text ganz ansprechend, vielleicht etwas marklos,
der nächste Schritt wäre dann
ein Kaninchenfell als Reichsflagge.

Persönlich unfruchtbar,
aber es wird schon werden.

And if you're given to talking about existential angst
some Midgard Serpent for breakfast,
the illimitable Oceanos in the evening,
and at night the being-thrown-into—then you'll sleep soundly—
the West no longer wants to defend itself—
it wants to be scared, it wants that thrown feeling.

A good pop song has more to say about 1950
than 500 pages of cultural crisis.
In the cinema, where you can keep your hat and coat with you,
there's more firewater than on the Kothurn,
and without the tedious delays.

(The quaternary was man turned in on himself,
now comes the triploid)
66 chromosomes, giant stature—

And as for the new national anthem!
The words pleasing, perhaps a little insipid,
the logical next step would be
running a bunny skin up the flagpole.

Personally unfruitful,
but I expect it'll happen.

Zeh war Apotheker
oder gab sich dafür aus,
Es waren friedliche Zeiten, man fragte nicht genau
aber als eine andre Woge kam „stellte man fest"
u das trug zu seinem Tode bei

Zeh zauberte ohne Gleichen
Pulver u Tabletten aus den Fächern
nicht daß er sie anpriese
man war von vornherein überzeugt
daß sie heilen würden.

Zeh hatte ein Entfettungsmittel gebraut
Zeean, das brauchte man kaum zu nehmen,
schon in der Tasche war es wirksam,
man schmolz schon hin.
Dies Gebräu der Apotheke hatte er an eins der Ladenfenster
    geklebt.

Was da sonst noch zu sehen war
an Kräutern, Mörsern, Dialogischen Hinweisen
für Tag- u Nachtereignisse unfälliger Art
war nicht zu schildern.
unübertrefflich *suggestiv*
psychosomatischer Hinsicht

Zeh was a pharmacist,
or claimed to be,
times were tranquil, people didn't ask too many questions,
but when a new broom came along, it was duly "established
   that" etc.
& it all contributed to his downfall

Zeh was an incomparable magician
shelves full of powders & tinctures
not that he had to sell them to you
you were persuaded of their efficacy
in advance.

Zeh had mixed up a slimming cure
called Zeean that you hardly even needed to take
it worked in your pocket
you straightaway started to reduce.
He had stuck that preparation in one of the pharmacy windows.

Among other things you could see there:
herbal teas, pestles and mortars, chatty tips
for di- & nocturnal events of an untoward nature
all of it defying description—
unrivaled in their suggestiveness
from a psychosomatic point of view

man würde ihn nie mehr auffinden
Kinder vacant
Grab längst weitervermietet

his like would never be found again
children (not likely!) *desunt,*
long since turfed out of his grave.

# RADIO

I

„– die Wissenschaft als solche" –
wenn ich derartiges am Radio höre,
bin ich immer ganz erschlagen.
Gibt es auch eine Wissenschaft nicht als solche?
Ich sehe nicht viel Natur, komme selten an Seen,
Gärten nur sporadisch, mit Gittern vor,
oder Laubenkolonien, das ist alles,
ich bin auf Surrogate angewiesen:
Radio, Zeitung, Illustrierte –
wie kann man mir da sowas bieten?

Da muß man doch Zweifel hegen,
ob das Ersatz ist für Levkoien,
für warmes Leben, Zungenkuß, Seitensprünge,
alles, was das Dasein ein bißchen üppig macht
und es soll doch alles zusammengehören!

Nein, diese vielen Denkprozesse sind nichts für mich,
aber es gibt volle Stunden,
wo man auf keinem Sender (Mittel-, Kurz-, Lang- und Ultrawelle)
eine Damenstimme hört („erst sagt man nein, dann vielleicht,
    dann ja"),

# RADIO

I

"—science per se"—
my God, when I hear them on the radio saying that,
it slays me.
Is there a science that's not per se?
I don't get out much, rarely get to see any lakes,
gardens only sporadically and then behind fences,
or in allotments, that's about the size of it,
I rely on ersatz:
radio, newspaper, magazines—
so how can people say such things to me?

It makes you wonder
whether there are any surrogates for hollyhocks,
for warm life, French kisses, hanky-panky,
all those things that make existence a little luxurious,
and all of them somehow of a piece!

No, all this cerebration is not my cup of tea,
but there are sometimes hours on end
where there's no woman on any wavelength
(I receive medium-wave, short-, long-, and VHF),
no voice saying, "first you say no, then maybe, then yes,"

immer nur diese pädagogischen Sentenzen,
eigentlich ist alles im männlichen Sitzen produziert,
was das Abendland sein Höheres nennt –
ich aber bin, wie gesagt, für Seitensprünge!


II


„– würden alte Kulturbestände völlig verschwunden sein –"
(nun, wenn schon)
„– klingende Vergangenheit –"
(von mir aus)
„– in den Orten Neu Mexikos
segnen die Farmer ihre Tiere und Felder
mit diesen Liedern –"
(angenehm,
aber ich meinerseits komme aus Brandenburg kaum heraus).

Wir hören Professor Salem Aleikum,
der Reporter beliebäugelt ihn noch:
„der Professor liegt auf der Terrasse seines Hauses
die Laute im Arm
und singt die alten Balladen" –
wahrscheinlich auf einer Ottomane,
Eiswasser neben sich,
widerlegt Hypothesen, stößt neue aus –

die größten Ströme der Welt
Nil, Brahmaputra oder was weiß ich,
wären zu klein, alle diese Professoren zu ersäufen –

nothing but these opinionated pedagogues,
it seems that everything the West thinks of as its
higher product is produced by the seated male—
as I say, give me the hanky-panky any day!


II


"—the last vestiges of the ancient culture would have completely
    disappeared—"
(well, and what if)
"—a sonorous past—"
(la-di-da)
"—in villages in New Mexico
farmers still bless their fields and livestock
with these songs—"
(very nice, I'm sure,
but I don't get out of Brandenburg much).


We hear Professor Salem Aleikum,
the reporter still slavering over him:
"the professor is lying on the porch of his house
with his lute cradled in his arm
singing the old ballads"—
probably on an ottoman,
with a carafe of ice water at his side,
rejecting old hypotheses, putting out new ones—

the great rivers of the world
the Nile, the Brahmaputra, or what the hell do I know
wouldn't be enough to drown all those professors—

ich habe kein Feld, ich habe kein Tier,
mich segnet nichts, es ist reiner Unsegen,
aber diese Professoren
sie lehren in Saus und Braus
sie lehren aus allen Poren
und machen Kulturkreis draus.

don't have any acreage, don't have any livestock,
nothing blesses me, life is one continuous affliction,
but nothing like those professors
teach, teach, teach,
from every pore,
who turn everything into illustrated lecture (with slides).

## DER GEDANKE

Der Gedanke —
anderthalb Meter reicht er,
eine Dose Daten erschleicht er,
aber sonst —?

Zum Beispiel Schafzucht,
ein Erdteil lebt davon,
dann kommen die Ersatzstoffe
und die Mufflons sind k.o.
Ursache: die asozialen Erfinder,
besessene Retortenchefs —
Fehltritte der Natur.

Oder die Wissenschaft
so eingleisig
ganz aus angelsächsischem Material.

Oder die Essaywelt,
einer webt den anderen ein
unter Aufsicht der Gewerkschaft.

„Sie kann man nicht mehr ernst nehmen" —
Gottseibeiuns — wunderbar!

## THINKING

Thinking—
has a reach of about four feet,
it can just about cope with one load of information at a time
but other than that?

Take sheepherding,
an entire continent lives by it,
then along come synthetic fibers
and the mouflons are *foutus*.
Cause: antisocial inventors,
obsessive test-tube johnnies—
nature's waifs and strays.

Or science
one-track, purposive
woven from Anglo-Saxon material.

Or take the essay world,
one man stitches up another
while the rest of the brotherhood looks on.

"It's simply not possible to take you seriously anymore"—
gawdhelpus—priceless knockabout!

Aber Eines ist die Wirklichkeit der Götter,
vielleicht aus trüben Quellen,
aber wenn sie da ist,
voll Erinnerung an Jene,

den Namen nenne ich nicht.

But there's one thought that is the reality of the gods,
its wellspring may indeed be murky,
but then it's there
full of memory of her

who shall remain nameless.

# AUFATMEN

Spannungen, Zerfallenheiten
direkt pelzgefüttert
und dann sieht man:

– – „Zwei gesunde Schnäpse trinken
kalte
klaren Köhm
das Bier heben
soliden Blicks
schaumgeboren
unzerstört ohne
Irritationen
Zwischenstufen
Abbauprodukte,
reiner Abendausklang
musikmitwiegend
etwas muffig, aber
gebißsicher
undunstig
unschwitzig
rückentrocken

Mitte des Lebens,
Fleisch, das die Nacht durchsteht

## BREATHE

Irritability, grief
positively fur-lined
and then you'll see:

"Knock back
a couple of shorts
good and cold
and clear
then raise your beer glass
steady eye
foam-born
intact
unalloyed
no half measures
or additives
pure yardarm
humming along
gruff (but when not)
teeth well cemented
no sweat or B.O.
dry-backed

prime of life
flesh that will make it through the night

schlafeingekränzt
reich behangen" – –

Aufatmen!

Bis wieder die Verlustziffern
Spannungen
Zerfallenheiten
direkt pelzgefüttert.

sleep-garlanded
richly festooned"

Now take a breath.

Till the onset of more losses
griefs
irritabilities
positively fur-lined.

## HÖR ZU:

Hör zu, so wird der letzte Abend sein,
wo du noch ausgehn kannst: du rauchst die „Juno",
„Würzburger Hofbräu" drei, und liest die Uno,
wie sie der „Spiegel" sieht, du sitzt allein

an kleinem Tisch, an abgeschlossenem Rund
dicht an der Heizung, denn du liebst das Warme.
Um dich das Menschentum und sein Gebarme,
das Ehepaar und der verhaßte Hund.

Mehr bist du nicht, kein Haus, kein Hügel dein,
zu träumen in ein sonniges Gelände,
dich schlossen immer ziemlich enge Wände
von der Geburt bis diesen Abend ein.

Mehr warst du nicht, doch Zeus und alle Macht,
das All, die großen Geister, alle Sonnen
sind auch für dich geschehn, durch dich geronnen,
mehr warst du nicht, beendet wie begonnen –
der letzte Abend – gute Nacht.

## LISTEN:

Listen, this is what the last evening will be like
when you're still capable of going out: you're smoking your Junos,
quaffing your three pints of Würzburger Hofbräu
and reading about the UN as reflected in the pages of the *Spiegel,*

you're sitting alone at your little table, the least possible company
beside the radiator, because you crave warmth.
All round you mankind and its mewling,
the married couple and their loathsome hound.

That's all you are, you've no house or hill
to call your own, to dream in a sunny landscape,
from your birth to this evening
the walls around you were always pretty tightly drawn.

That's all you were, but Zeus and all the immortals,
the great souls, the cosmos and all the suns
were there for you too, spun and fed through you,
that's all you were, finished as begun—
your last evening—good night.

# 1953

Ein Tag ohne Tränen ist ein Zufall
eine Gedankenlosigkeit
schon eine Manie

*

Als man noch schlechte Kragenknöpfe hatte
mit Schmerzen hinkte, um die Zehen Watte
da man noch nichts von Pedicure geahnt
       angebahnt
u fand Gesichter, die man noch bestaunte
es waren Jahre, wo noch etwas raunte

## FRAGMENTS 1953

A day without tears is a rare occurrence
culpable absentmindedness
practically an episode

&ast;

When men still wore starched collars,
and stuffed cotton wool between their toes
hobbled about in pain, pedicure hadn't been invented,
but you would see faces that were worth a second look
those were years when something whispered

# 1955

30 x unter Qualen die Zähne plombieren lassen
100 x Rosen aus dem Süden gehabt
4 x an Gräbern geweint
25 Frauen verlassen
2 x die Tasche voll Geld u 98 x ohne Geld gehabt,
Schließlich tritt man in eine Versicherung ein mit
12 50 pro Monat um
seine Beerdigung sicher zu stellen

*

Oder die 3 Takte von Tschaikowsky
die man durch 3 Etagen erkennt

*

was bist Du? Ein Symptom
ein Affe ein Gnom –

eingenistet in die Sommerstunde
das Gewürz von                    u Wald –

## FRAGMENTS 1955

30x endured agonies at the dentist's
100x treated myself to expensive imported roses
4x shed tears beside open graves
left 25 women
2x had a pocket full of money & 98x not,
at the end of the day you take out an insurance policy
at 12.50 per month,
to be certain of being buried

   *

Or those 3 bars of Tchaikovsky
that you recognize 3 floors away

   *

what are you? A symptom,
an ape, a gnome—

nestling in the summer,
the freshness of         & forest—

*prose*

## EPILOGUE 1921

Born in 1886 to a Lutheran clergyman and a Frenchwoman from Yverdon, Switzerland, in a village of three hundred souls roughly halfway between Berlin and Hamburg, grew up in a similar-sized village in Brandenburg. Went to boarding school, then university, studied languages and theology for two years, then switched to medicine at the Kaiser Wilhelm Academy; was an active army doctor in provincial regiments, invalided out when a kidney got loose in the course of a six-hour gallop; continued my medical training, went to America, inoculated the steerage; the War began, stormed Antwerp, lived behind the lines, hanging out in Brussels with Sternheim, Flake, Einstein, and Hausenstein; currently in Berlin as a specialist for sexually transmitted diseases; consultation hours on weekday evenings, from 5 to 7.

I took my license as a doctor, researched, wrote papers on diabetes in the army, vaccinations for gonorrhea, peritonitis, cancer statistics, received the Gold Medal from the University of Berlin for some research on epilepsy; what I composed by way of literature was written, apart from *Morgue*, which was published by A. R. Meyer in 1912, in the spring of 1916 in Brussels. I was a doctor in a hospital for prostitutes, a very isolated post, lived in a sequestrated villa, shared eleven rooms with my orderly, had little to do, was allowed to wear civvies, wasn't bothered with anything, wasn't attached to anyone, hardly understood the language; wandered through the streets, among strangers; a strange spring, three incomparable months, every day I heard the bombardment on the Yser, what did I care, life was bounded in a sphere of silence and lostness, I lived on the edge where existence ceases and the self begins. I often think back on those weeks; they were life, they'll not come back, everything else was garbage.

Insofar as I can judge four thousand years of human history, it seems to me there are two types of neurological reactions. Differentiated by their sense of the relationship among parts and the whole, their response to the notion of totality. On the one hand: primacy of the whole, *to hen kai pan*, chance play of forms, painful and centripetal; Indian, speculative, introverted; expressionist. And on the other: absolute of the active individual, with the concept as inventory: casuists, activists, ethical and muscular. I am with the holists, the chaos merchants, to such a degree that to me Darwin is a midwife and the ape is arts and crafts: we invented space to kill time, and time for our boredom; nothing is evolving or happening, the category in which the cosmos is revealed is the category of stagnation.

I am the product of a scientific century; I know my condition all too well. Bacchanal through singularities, concretism triumphal, then multiply broken under the laws of stylization and synthetic function, averted in my centers, a grotesque persiflage; and I must add here that I was not always engaged in the skin trade either. I was a psychiatrist until I was affected by a peculiar and worsening syndrome that eventually left me unable to summon any interest in the individual case.

It was physically not possible for me to focus my attention, my interest on a new case, or to continue to observe old cases while respecting individual particulars. Questions as to the genesis of a malady, establishing a patient's background and way of life, tests applied to the individual's intelligence and moral alertness, all caused me indescribable torments. My mouth dried, my eyelids reddened, I might have resorted to violence if my boss hadn't called me in, complained about my completely inadequate record-keeping, and sacked me.

I strove to understand the nature of my affliction. From the psychiatry textbooks where I began looking, I came to current psychological works, some of them very odd, especially those of the French school; I immersed myself in descriptions of the condition known as depersonalization, or alienation from the perceptual world, I began to see the self as a construct that, with a force to which gravity was like the puff of a snowflake, strove for a condition in which nothing of what modern culture saw as intellection played any role, only that which civilization—in the form of school medicine—had tended to dismiss as nervous, easily tired, psychasthenic: the admission of a deep, endless, myth-old estrangement between human beings and the world.

Impossible still to exist in any community, impossible to depend on it in life or calling; too transparent the ricketiness of its antithetical structure, too contemptible the perpetual coital compromise of crude antinomies . . . I had read in Montesquieu that Caligula, being descended from Antony on the one side and Augustus on the other, promised to punish his Consuls if they celebrated the anniversary of the battle of Actium, but equally would punish them if they failed to celebrate it; and when

Drusilla, to whom he had given divine honors, died, it was accounted a crime to mourn her because she was a goddess, and not to mourn her, as his sister. I had that in mind. That was what I thought of whenever I came up against the contemporary. That was how I saw him, whichever way he tried to propose himself to me; it was the "on the one hand" and "on the other hand" structure wherever he went, the professional-diagonal as sexual prophylactic. On the one hand and on the other hand: the most committed individualist to the dirt under his fingernails, and forced to social compromises from feeding to sexual habits; always that mediocre balance, and that tediously positive latency. Lemurs, shapes, screeching nightmares, with the void slithering around their galoshes; words, Horatio, movements of the lips, blowing seed into chitchat, I lowered my portcullis and locked my doors, and went on my travels, and kept having to go back, having failed to find a desert in Europe. A gentleman sits in my waiting room, he directs his speech to me, the sum of the experiences of an estimable life play about his lips, he seeks to purchase curative substances from me; courage, friend, things will improve, calm, sedation. I look across the street, a gentleman is brushing the dust off his coat, but at this moment a good many gentlemen are brushing the dust off their coats, wherever you look, always this simultaneity, back and forth between stabilization and the wide and unquestioning, between concept and absolute, back and forth . . .

How is one to live? Of course, one isn't. Vasomotorically labile, neurotically incontinent, ecce in the morgue and ecce in the apocalypse, schizothymia in lieu of affect, abortions in every direction instead of fertility, autopsychically solitary, lazily monocular, Polyphemus among the sheep with their bounty strapped to their bellies; thirty-five and completely wiped out, I don't write anymore—one would have to write with coprolalia and intestinal worms; don't read anymore—or who do you suggest I read? The honest old Titans with their Icarus wings in grease-proof paper? I think no thought through to its conclusion—adorable the picture of Western man, still and all till the Occident sinks in shadow, stepping out to meet chaos with the one weapon at his disposal, the concept, the sling, David-like to fight for his life—but forget about tactics, I have a glimmering of existence outside the antithetical psychology of perennially latent syndicalist metaphysics.

Now these complete works, one volume, two hundred pages, thin stuff, one would be ashamed if one were still alive. No document worthy the name; I would be astonished if anyone were to read them; to me they are already very distant, I toss them behind me like Deucalion his stones; maybe human beings will emerge from the gargoyles; but whether they do or not, I shan't love them.

The north of France, which one passes through on the way to Paris from Berlin, is flat; it might be Friesland or Jutland; the Seine basin, nowhere girdled by any substantial hills. It contains places one would sooner forget: Maubeuge, Charleville, Laon, Compiègne; in St. Quentin the cathedral looms bulkily and rather lewdly; standing there with its lofty, blue-gray naked thighs in the razed countryside. Then Champagne, very poor, no woods, no arable land, all grazing, no villages; but the chalk slopes incomparably well tended for the world-famous *mousseux*.

Between the Pyrenees and the Ardennes is the greatest wine-producing region of Europe; the value of the annual yield is put at two hundred and seventy million francs, divided among two hundred and fifty vintages; in bulk terms, France supplies forty million buckets per annum, Germany manages four and a half, Spain eight and a half; in Paris the amount per head or gorge of population is one hundred and twelve liters a year. In addition, France is the most splendid fruit-growing country in Europe, and between Cannes and Grasse flowers are grown the way other places turn out barley and rutabagas. Per year two million pounds of orange blossoms are harvested, one and a half million pounds of roses, seventy-five thousand pounds of violets, lavender and rosemary are as abundant as grass and clover in our breadths.—This is where the little places are that spread intoxicating smells over miles and miles, the factories of the famous firms that keep their head offices in the rue de la Paix.

If you put Berlin's Kurfürstendamm and Unter den Linden together, and multiply the sum by, say, a factor of ten, then there are about twenty such streets in front of you when you stand with your back to the Madeleine. On your right is a shop selling nothing but blue ostrich feathers, on your left is one selling only pearls. Stockings, vertically striated in three colors, melting into each other like the bands of the rainbow will be this summer's hit. For the moment it is still the cape trimmed with ermine. In cloaks dimensioned like theater curtains, closed with one hand flashing a diamond the size of a hazelnut, the ladies step into the restaurant at midnight after the theater. The oysters are from Portugal, they have long beards and scant flesh, but what there is is firm and salty. The olives are plump with Tarasconian oil; the poulards, softened by heavy Burgundian sauces, are melting off the bone; champagne is poured over pistachio ices; anyone not in tails is a boor. There's Potin, the food store. But what food, what a store! Wertheim for delicacies, three blocks in Moorish style to a pile of Canaanite drapes. Pilasters, suffocating in pineapples; pillars, green with figs and artichokes; an indoor stream for trout; snipe and pheasant in rows, ricks of asparagus, a pyramid of plovers' eggs, cakes out onto the pavement. Paris gets through twenty thousand hectoliters of olive oil a year for its salads and mayonnaises—while we, "Jean Potage," chomp our sauerkraut.

Or there's the Moulin Rouge. Carpets of a particular shade of red between salmon and glacé cherries are laid from the pavements up the stairs into every recess of the theater. In one corner there's a Dixie band from Red River, in the other, a shark-charmer from Colombo. And onstage there is New York / Montmartre, la grande Revue du Moulin Rouge, two acts, fifty scenes, sixty creators, all individually credited, including the authors, the buckles on the shoes, the mother of pearl on the shell dancers, and the manager of the telephonists.

It's my belief that the budget of the Prussian state wouldn't be able to finance this revue. Every continent has been plundered. The man from Chinatown has just the right jerky movements and the mystique of the East opens up before our eyes. The Iroquois hisses menacingly, the tomahawk bites, and there's the melancholy twang of the Wild West. And dance, dance, dance. Gradually become insufferable in the rest of Europe, here thrilling, off-color and elegant: Buck Dance, Flicker Dance, Peacock's Mirror Dance, Jazz Dance, Leopard Dance, Danse des Gigolettes, Danse des Candélabres.—And pictures, continents, cultures; things rising up out of trapdoors, other things spilling out of bonbon boxes, riding, driving, leaps into the Nile, family scenes, Black Masses, ball on the roof of the Astor, Temptations of St. Antony, Panther Column of the Queen of Sheba: Apaches, magicians, standard-bearers, lotus wearers, catamites, amazons, and—"*ah, viens dans mes bras*"—slaves.

Paris is Palmyra where the purple grew, the harbor of Sluys where one hundred and fifty merchant vessels docked in the space of an hour, the Bruges of that Brabant where the pregnant mothers in the surrounding provinces betook themselves in the week they were due: so that their babies might get a share of the wealth of that city. It's the storehouse of the world and the mess of nations; in its endless complexity it has acquired incomparable treasures; in its blackened streets it has a reek of the world that is more intoxicating than New York's.

It's not technology, not automobiles, not sheer scale that drives the masses. In Tauentzienstraße, if you see a couple of limousines one after the other, and a bus in the distance, that constitutes heavy traffic. Here you might get five or six taxis racing down the boulevards, line abreast, with the same number going the other way, no speed limits are given or adhered to, it's a straightforward race; anyone who sets foot on the road without police assistance is tired of life; it's not the dimensions of the buildings, though the Louvre and the Palais-Royal, from centuries when Paris had a couple of hundred thousand inhabitants, even now seem to exceed the requirements of a city of four million; it's not the four thousand rarities in the museums, or the stained glass of the Sainte-Chapelle; no one can deny that Berlin is a booming city, but Paris is the genius of the French nation, which it brings to expression at any moment.

Since the time of the Capetians it's been the city of arts, since the Bourbon centuries, of money, the city of Napoléon in its luster and swagger. Nothing is past, everything is still current: history takes up the contemporary and toys with it. Yes, the Pantheon is a somewhat academic Valhalla, but at the feet of Joan of Arc, on the pediment of the glum little shepherdess, are eighteen bouquets, some fresh, some a little withered. How often she came to life before her country, "the most beautiful under the sun": at noon when the flower girl brought her violets, or the couple took her a little bunch of primroses at evening. How often the youngest appear at the sites of old renown: in the Comédie Française flanked by Molière and Corneille the statues of a couple of twenty-five-year-olds who lost their lives at Laon or on the Marne; what will they have achieved in their years?— no more than their German contemporaries, but I never heard of Franz Marc or Alfred Lichtenstein or Georg Trakl being offered so much as a laurel wreath around their names.

It's the city of pomp, of antiques, of porcelain, of jewels and an insatiable love of fashion. But all this luxury doesn't come over as exclusive, which is curious. It's a lavish nation; well, in the course of so many centuries of conquest, it has acquired the wherewithal. The allure is that of style, which acquires its uniqueness by exaggeration: the empty automatism of technology has won a soulful magic by the imposition of luxury over need. It's a mistake to think that savages are the better humans. Whoever doubts, let him consult Schiller, whose history of the Low Countries absolved the waste, the pleasure, the prodigality of the Burgundian court: "to the friend of humanity how much more joyful this excess than the wretchedness of sufficiency and the barbaric virtue of stupidity, under which most of Europe groaned at the time."

Is Paris anti-German? I didn't notice it. Things are where they belong. In the courtyard of the Invalides, on the left-hand side, on the original rails, ringed by hundred German mortar throats, the wagon of Maréchal, in which he "*imposait*" the terms of the Armistice on November 11, 1918, at five in the morning, in Franc-Port; the German signatories were Erzberger, von Winterfeld, Vanselow. But then the Invalides is the army museum. There is a strange trophy not far from there: an old Parisian hackney cab, draped with the flags of the Entente. Its story is as follows: in September 1914, at the time of the Battle of the Marne, there was not enough transport to take the troops to the front. Taxis were requisitioned. Paris had no cars left, an unimaginable notion. The taxis are old and small, at the most two or three men will go inside with their gear; they will have plastered themselves over the outside, like so many bees. And so they drove to the Front. They are old structures, the long drive will not have done them much good. And now one has been placed in the museum, with the *tricoleur* unfurled over its battered chassis.

But that's the emotional life of arsenals. In the city itself, there are no traces of war and victory—unlike in Italy, for instance, where each village has a war memorial to its heroes, with flags and swords and Fascist slogans. The German visitor is completely unmolested in the city, even if he's reading a German newspaper. On the bus, I heard two fellow nationals talking together in the overloud way we have, waving their sticks around—no one seemed to notice. In the shops you are addressed in French, English, and German, in that order, if communication is not immediately established. The kiosks stock numerous German newspapers: at one I saw the *Berliner Tageblatt, Vossische Zeitung, Deutsche Allgemeine Zeitung, Tag, Rote Fahne, Frankfurter Zeitung, Hannoversche Kurier*, and *Weltbühne*. The Frankfurt Fair is advertised on many streets: "Foire de Francfort." In the Grand Opéra they perform Wagner at least twice a week, in French, and the performances are sold out. I went to a concert by a Russian soprano, whose current engagement at the Berliner Staatsoper was in no way swept under the carpet. In the *Figaro* I read an enthusiastic review of the Nibelungen film that has just come out. Numerous German films starring German actors are announced; on one page of the *Journal* the names Krauß, Steinrück, Veit, and Lucie Mannheim all leapt out at me. In general, one has the sense that the old generation, those in their seventies, the Clémenceau generation, thinks differently; but youth is mobile and uncomplicated as young people are the world over.

What about the arts? How are the opera and theater? Less interesting than in Berlin. *Hedda Gabler* at the Comédie Française, apparently no standby of the Parisian: *très bizarre*, my neighbor kept exclaiming, *très bizarre*! Hedda's mime was good, the most irritable face I have ever seen on a woman, but her acting was 1880s naturalistic salon drama; Lövborg a sentimental chatterbox, floppy necktie for stiff collar as a sign of social decline; the rest all tubercular poets.—A brace of Pirandellos in a theater in the suburbs, experimental stage in Montmartre, unknown to all hotel porters I asked. To go by the program, Pirandello's earliest play, *Chacun sa vérité (Così è)*, the same kitsch problem with Pilate nonsense. *What Is Truth?* like the *Six Characters* with a touch of devilment about it, but harder, punchier, tenser, pushed through three acts and with two plum roles, the production really quite *épatant*. In the Grand Opéra, *Le crépuscule des dieux* and *La Valkyrie* would not have impressed them in Bayreuth: the acting was Meyerbeer and the singing Puccini. The voices no better than average, Wotan a well-tempered lounge demon, Brünnhilde the elegant lyric soprano, the entire final scene aria'ed from the prompt box into the audience without attention to Grane, her horse, and the circling ravens, while the funeral pyre stacked on the banks of the Rhine seemed more like the lighting for a mead soirée than the debacle of a mythological world. But one may be permitted to observe that the countless German lads and lasses monologizing about their drastic sexual needs between rues Pigalle and Lafayette are not exactly *chic* either.

Last summer, Paris hosted the Olympics, this year they are holding an international show of arts and crafts; every nation except Germany and Norway has its white house. The craziest products and achievements are paraded and compared, a few will be chosen, the rest will sink from memory, the world will knot itself into new fashions and forms, now they will be swanning down Broadway, now down the gold-washing towns of Virginia. Then they will be finished, and it will be over. But one way or another they will return to Paris, one of the mothers of the world, la grande Isis, the diadem city.

That's Paris, taken at a rush, Lutetia, city of fever, city of dreams. From the Bois de Boulogne the wind blows through the Tuileries round the obelisk of Sesostris and the planes flanking the statue of Charlemagne. Thirty bridges over the Seine, and the Arc de Triomphe and the genius of a people and underneath it the heart of the *inconnu*. City of love and of pools of blood, of crowned heads and Communards, city of paupers and of famous men—*ah, viens dans mes bras!*

## SUMMA SUMMARUM 1926

So much is being done for the arts again these days, no beer evening is complete without their representatives, scribblers are invited to the ministry, potters pot and weavers weave, learned allusions are made to the banks of the Arno. My offering is strictly numerical, a tally, an analysis of how much I earned from poetry and miscellaneous authorship in the course of my life. At the time of my first publication, I was twenty-five years old, this month I turned forty, what is at issue are fifteen years, and I have scrupulously totted up everything I earned from books (including a collected works), articles, reprints, anthology rights, in a word, anything to do with the printing and publishing industry: the total comes to 975 marks.

So far as poetry goes, I earned 40 marks for a lyric pamphlet published by my friend Alfred Richard Meyer in 1913, another 20 marks for poems in Schickele's *Weiße Blätter* during the war, and after the war 30 marks for two poems in *Querschnitt*, that makes 90 marks for poetry. Unlike my friend Else Lasker-Schüler, I don't have to clean up, my medical specialism has so far paid the bills. And even though venereal diseases seem to be disappearing from the face of the earth, and an international congress of syphilodologists in 1925 in Paris has estimated that over the last five years the incidence of lues has retreated by 50 percent in Europe, I harbor no particular grudge against

Ehrlich-Hata. As I say, this is a back-of-the envelope reckoning of writing and thinking, a statistically based reflection on art and life and the Muses' spring.

Before I go on, I must make one more prefatory remark. It makes no difference to what follows whether my literary reputation is more or less just, or whether I am criminally over- or underestimated. The figures are what they are:

On and with and included in these 975 marks are translations into the French, English, Russian, and Polish, and appearances in anthologies in the USA, France, and Belgium. The last year has seen the publication of articles or remarks on me in Paris in the *Nouvelles littéraires*, *Volonté*, and *L'opinion républicaine*, so far as I know. I read a review by the French author Reber of a French survey of German literature, which he took a dim view of because it failed to deal with figures like myself. In a lecture given at the Sorbonne, M. Soupault counted me among the top five poets not just in Germany, but in all Europe. In a single week in March I received a copy of an essay on me from Paris; I had a visit from a journalist come from Warsaw to interview me; and I had a request from Moscow for my photograph and CV for an international art exhibition. Or should I be embarrassed to list these things? But that's celebrity, the same everywhere! The literary historians in Germany count me among the most prominent expressionist poets, the wireless accorded me a full hour-long installment of its *Stunde der Lebenden* with and contrasted with—*sit venia comparationi*—Stefan George, and a newspaper described me on this occasion as "one of the great men of the age."

Now let me compare these 975 marks with the earnings of

others in the creative and intellectual industries. A good solo dancer gets 300 marks an evening for her appearances in the Staatsoper, an averagely known film actor earns 400 per day of a shoot, the first violin in a respectable festival orchestra clears 1,500 a month, the conductor of the orchestra at the Marmorhaus cinema 4,000. Not wishing to compare myself to actresses of modest gifts and steady engagements, who are certain to make 2,000 marks a month, and leaving out of account the salaries of editors, managers, and bank directors, and the boardroom rates paid to parliamentarians, when I so much as think of the lyric tenor in Königsberg or the Wotan in Karlsruhe hauling in his two or three thousand a month, then one of the great men of the age is looking just a bit seedy on his 4.50 an hour.

But as I say, I'm not complaining. To complain would be to find fault with the social order, and I think the social order is dandy. Think of them fearlessly making their way out of the darkness into the light. Those politicians and ministers, making rhetorical mileage out of the Whitsun miracle and the Apocalypse, and when they die, the great, grieving household names of companies take space to lament their passing. Those literary heroes, every day an interview—does anyone really think that if they were talking about piles or Kukirol for corns, they would sound any *less* ostentatious? Those arty-farty periodicals: "What have you got on the stocks at the moment?" and then those knights witter on about their aesthetics in terms compared to which a decent cobbler's thoughts on lasts would be a profound human utterance. Those questionnaires: "In what chapter do you think it's appropriate for the hero to pop the question?" and none of those solicited send in their answer in the form of a matchbox full of sputum—no, leave me to go on giving my injections for gonorrhea, 20 marks cash in hand, no toothache, no corns, everything else is community, and I steer clear of that.

Or what is there speaks for community? Kleist in Machnow reaching for the revolver, or Uncle Fritz at the end of his life, greetings from Sils Maria, when he stayed with his sister and allowed his beard to sprout, or Weininger or the *morituri* at Calvary, vinegar dabbed on their adenoids and their feet bathed in the tears of two old crones—and then the beer evenings with the fellows! Machnow, Golgotha, all for 4.50, but I go to my gonorrhea patients, and a new poem every month! A poem is the unpaid labor of the intellect, the *fonds perdu*, practice with a sandbag: one-sided, inconsequential, and without partners— *evoe!*

## THE SEASON 1930

Late fall, early season. Flicker of openings and premières. *Heure bleue* compounded from Spree River mists and gaslights, further twilit by the rush-hour traffic. Gleaming onset of the world's neurosis: true-life crashes and sporting upsets, pattering accelerando of promissory notes and credit collapses, septic terrain, subfebrile crises.

Night falls, entertainment kicks in, the moral institutions open their portals, the art temples offer up their Holy of Holies. Eight o'clock, here come the Packards and beside them the Chryslers, one chauffeur in royal blue, one page in mint green, the foyers favored equally by state and industry fill with the great and the good, with the entitled and the self-entitled, the top drawer as well as the foothills of culture. Senior figures in government and finance, the gentlemen have just flogged an entire branch of industry abroad for 500 million at 6 percent over fifty years; the board of our biggest and newest brass works, the session has just ended where they voted, heavily indebted, to offer 25 percent of the stock to the chemical industry in London, ceding control of the company, but extremely lucrative to the individuals concerned; the ex-minister whose superb connections throughout industry and politics make him such an invaluable consultant to the big banks; the great coryphée, the doctor, of whom it is said in the Widsom of Sirach that the Lord made him, but who this afternoon was lucky enough to sell his name to a corsetmaker, The Bouncing Belles; the owner of the biggest west German flour wholesaler, currently 13 million under, owing to some little mishap involving credit swaps—they all beat a path to the arts, to choral singing, to the tragic buskin. Nor is the representative of the so-called National Idea far to seek, who, having embezzled 8 million of state funds, has no more need to breathe the unhealthy asphalt air; or the ex officio administrator of wardship moneys, who—belatedly, one would have thought— has remembered himself and siphoned off a trifling 3 million to keep body and soul together; a few of the forty city officials who brokered building deals among themselves with 100-mark handshakes; the defense attorney who smuggled the pen and special ink into his client's prison cell so that he—for Auld Lang Syne— might write out a few more dodgy IOUs to pay his legal bills— they all are seeking clarity and calm and consolation in the word resounding from the boards, in the cleansing atmosphere of moral sentiments, in the loftiness of ethical struggle.

A hush now comes over the stalls. At the front on the free seats are the critics, puffed up by vanity; whether the provincial tenor switches his bulk to the ball of his left or right foot, whether Miss Parsunke's cry comes from the depths of passion or the height of her cleft palate, matters to them because thereby hangs their position in the editorial office, their indispensableness to the paper. Flanking them, a sprinkling of our great novelists, never anything under eight hundred pages a pop, astounding rate of production, the density of invention and imagination, surely they should be made to carry baskets, toss in a few cod, and they could be so many fishwives. The lights go dark. The intellectual

justification for scene-shifters and the diva's costume changes—
or play—gets under way. The husband has a mistress, but his
wife, ballsy modern woman that she is, is determined to win him
back. Enter a young man, a beach acquaintance from Biarritz:
"Germaine, do you remember that evening? I wanted you so
badly, but you refused. Not now, some other time, you said." Now
he's put to work, he's the cat's-paw, a little light is spilled on him
too, or rather on his parts, but primarily his function is to dig the
dramatic hole a little deeper, also for the woman to sic him onto
her rival, and finally for Fate, which will lead the woman to the
edge of the abyss ("It's so hot here, Aristide, won't you help me
off with my jacket"), from which at the last moment, principally
from overtiredness of the partner, she retreats. The fight is over,
the crisis is solved, Mr. and Mrs. Smith clinch, they make plow-
shares not swords, the night ends in married whisperings. The
claque that applauds is as bad as the claque that boos, there are
imbeciles on the right and imbeciles on the left, tomorrow they
will applaud a tomato prophet, the day after a ventriloquist, no
matter, why ever not, brain rot, crap, God's tank.

Truly the arts are a people's finest flowering, to listen to the
exiting conversations, what a noble performance, but now we re-
turn to the *actualité*, China, gentlemen, is where the action is,
yes, the Americans may have cornered the market in cigarettes,
but lenses and cameras have been earmarked for Germany,
400 million inhabitants, what if one in ten start taking pictures,
that's still 40 million. Say cheese, happy days! The ladies to their
graphologists: "With you it's telepathy, mine only needs to put
his hand in his trouser pocket, then he's farsighted"—they glit-
ter, and reach for their hat pins. The parliamentarians, draped

like creepers over the boxes for no extra charge, noble tribunes of the people, free travelers, lobby fodder, each catch in the voice a check of the bank balance, each pause for breath an invoice in the post. The press—well, look at us: guttersnipes, scum, homosexually begotten bastard tortoises, wide boys whose mothers forgot themselves with well-situated editors, feuilleton chiefs, wood-pulp ennoblers—and if it wasn't about places on the board, then it was about forest acres: Count Collalto's pile in Vienna with its 30,000 square meters of parkland has just gone into the portfolio of one of their own.

And next to the temples of the Muses are the frontages of Minerva, because art and science are a people's twin supports, the true and the beautiful, frescoed on the wall in the foyer of every academy, in every plenary room. One figure looks up and out, into the Open, the Ideal, with hair unbound; the other looks down, with a stylus or dividers in her hand, and then something hard, usually round, a globe or skull. Statuary too, the *de rigueur* Titan, Lucifer *in profundis*, all the vagaries of nature from Babylon to Timbuctoo, all its mistakes, but now, at this hour, packed with men of learning: what pleasure merely to stand there and look and wait—let's join them.

At the moment, Minerva is busy with Aurignac, Darwin's obverse, we are all merely symbolic. She is also busy with her hair: because with a hair, she divides the fertilized egg, isolates the two halves, studies the fate of the parted rudiments, frogs are bred, front end tree frog, back end swamp frog, melded together, they would say, at an early embryonic stage. Individuals, free living beings, are produced from spare parts. The Lycian Chimera pales before these glorious malformations, whose crowning triumph is the mélange of frog and newt. Moreover, we can make eyes, produce eyes, build eyes, but might not that be from some force, some energy outwith the lab, some suprainductive, transempirical, extraexperimental background? For God's sake, man, bite your tongue, we may be wearing the casual line from *Nisus formativus* Caspar Friedrich Wolff via Driesch's entelechy to Spemann's synergetic principle—but there is more at stake than science and understanding here: this is about endowed chairs and career advancement—with those feather dusters of the split hair, those *avantageurs* of eyesight!

Aside from the wheelbase, which, according to the promotional material, is far longer than one should expect for such a price, and way past the International Women's Congress (the most important result of whose recently ended session was the formation of a committee to look into the possibilities of future meetings), science this winter is bringing the acausal nature of history. Physical laws are, ahem, merely statistical probabilities. Physicists and philosophers are united in taking the absolute determinism of the atomic process for "unlikely"; one of the most universal formulas, the so-called Second Law of Thermodynamics, or the entropy formula, which is involved in every physical process, turns out to be the prototype of a statistical law. Cracks in the structure, splits in the hymen, a ghost in the Parthenon, the worm in consolidated property; the truth has become a swizz, pale ale; Pilate's washing water has become a rippling rill—but, hey, here's to the new Navy League, Pseudo Galileo, Bogus Copernicus, Peer-Review Newton—the brain-mâché of the little burgher!

There he stands, the narrow little man- and animal-head,

thinking, whiffling, woolgathering—it doesn't occur to anyone that the medieval luminaries were no members of learned societies, no massed ranks of professors, no suppliers of factory secrets, actually no scientists at all, but unpaid demons: "rather sleep on oxhides than on dignity and respect," while all this here, fully a hundred years from the last echt intellectual breakthrough, pampered by a century of liberalism and ease; with instruments, formulas, textbooks that it has inherited or purchased, following recipes that it carries on gurgitating and regurgitating, its casuistical underpinning vital at most for an exam candidate, inflated into a philosophy of life, swilled with the help of press and photographers into the color magazines and soigné evening classes to persuade a wider public ("tomorrow a ventriloquist, the day after the tomato gospel") of its relevance; a bureaucracy of research scientists assorted by pay grade, an international civilization guild with full pension rights that could perfectly well be replaced en bloc by an equal number of grad students and an equal number of hemorrhoids.

In intellectual and social terms this is the prototype of the age: no experience and no essence; charged with establishing the truth but only when truth is what can be established, a notarized calculation (with "working out" shown), complete with potential rates of return for investors. At home they might collect stamps, stroke the violin, and fill bush and valley; then they might get a little stir-crazy, as creators, demiurges, cosmic shudders in their pigeon chests. So, at eight o'clock at night they step into the moral institutions, the temples of art, and the foyers equally favored by state and public. At ten o'clock it's over, the theaters as they say, let out, the soigné evening classes dismiss.

It's early yet, they say, it's a mild night. There they are adrift among all this humanity, whose intellectual cream they are, to whom they explain everything so plausibly, and make industry so gosh-darn cheap. Night over this Western pleasure precinct, this rutting zone, this glandular Palmyra—venturesome flotsam from the deep shade to the flashing blue light, criminals and deviants, psychotics and bankrupts, barflies, butt bandits, frigid swamp honeys—instinct sliced and diced from the Dome to the Rotonda.

Brains melted by toxins distilled from all manner of flora and fauna, the lethal factors of an overrefined race potentiated, awash with pleasure hormones—over Malay cocktails mixed over the Atlantic, lazy, sluttish, and pauperized the midshipman of the Mitropa junk. In front of him, life jitterbugs away. The soybean, completely unknown to the European market as recently as 1909, is today baked into its daily bread, 900,000 tons of it ground to flour; 8,000 different medicines are churned out by the chemical industry, all of them leaching into the nation's lymph system. Sugar consumption has risen steeply, preference in meat has moved, with profound economic consequences, from dark, indigestible beef and game to pallid fish and poultry. Science has drawn the bitterness from the lupin, thickened the ear of wheat, perfected the crumb cake, and everything else is taken care of by the professional organization: nurses' teats, pacifiers, corpse washing—all of it communal.

The genitals are no longer taken seriously, except their diseases; all that's left of convictions is the dividend they pay. Four hundred million mice weigh as much as a full-grown hippopotamus, but they eat as much as a herd of rhinos, which makes mouse feed a sexy proposition. So come on lads, get into mouse feed, the lab bosses have cooked up a little analysis, with a press release, etc.—nutritional data, nationwide campaign, trained sales force, all God's children, seen the woods and sniffed the air, and when they suddenly cash in their chips, there are three ironed shirts left in the wardrobe. O Enlightenment, O Progress, O Induction—with 30 public lavatories and 890 research institutes, they bred the new metropolitan race. Brain, brain on cortical day-release, a formula for business and an insole for fallen arches, but remember to wash your mouth out after kissing— O Aurignac, which saw off four ice ages, and painted its caves with fantastical elephants' hearts, in the momentum of a fallen buffalo your great troglodytic heart lived 50,000 years—now, before your offshoots, so overbred that the skulls bulge and the quills wreck the pelvises: abortion motets, the minstrel tic-tactoes his bungalow, a Neanderthal jazz band hymns Africa, and the Red River spills new life and new death all over your brushes and pipettes.

## RILKE 1940

Rilke larded the pages of his correspondence with the names of aristocrats who owned—just imagine—a very nice collection of old *livres d'heures*, and landed estates, and a castle in the Ukraine, and a stud for thoroughbred Arab horses, all that somehow didn't sound quite so stifling at the time, even though the letters were addressed to countesses, and were written in palaces, or at the very least on paper headed Villa des Brillants, Meudon-Val Fleury (Seine et Oise), supplied with date and time of day. Or again, the richness of his nature, from which all this correspondence flowed, might call for the following bulletin: "On Saturday, 1 June, I took my first ever Turkish bath with entire pleasure, and not a smidgeon of unease. It was a wonderful feeling, to be seated in that goodly warmth, for which I was prepared by our own *chaleur*, yes, I even wished there might be more of it waiting for me outside the baths." A hot bath, Meudon, and then even that is found to be too bracing—cue creative crisis, and three months in Capri or Viareggio, which he spends in plusfours, "so to speak, bare-legged," and: "a little chime set up in me, perhaps quite faint after so much time, therefore it didn't seem a good idea to me to entrust this sounding-bowl to the big railway train, and head off to new impressions in Genoa and Dijon, and more advisable to wait out the birth, howsoever inconsequential, here." Something quite faint and a goodly warmth, a compound of virile dirt and lyrical depth, pampered by duchesses, poured out in letters to the broad-hipped Ellen Key— so much for the annus mirabilis of 1907. Happy Fatherland! In the end, everything comes up roses, another castle is found, from where he addresses the poor, hears god, and ruffles the poultry coop. That frail figure and repository of great poetry, dead from leukemia, bedded among the bronze hills of the Rhône valley in a *terroir* where French is spoken, wrote the line my generation will never forget: "Who speaks of victory—survival is all!"

## BLOCK II, ROOM 66 1944

was the address of the quarters where I was billeted for a number of months. The barracks was situated high over the town like a fortress. Montsalvat, remarked one first lieutenant, who was familiar with grand opera, and indeed it had little to offer to the casual stroller: once you'd made your way from the railway station to the foot of the hill, you had one hundred and thirty-seven steps left to climb.

Nothing so dreamy as barracks! Room 66 looks out onto the exercise yard, in front of it are three small rowan trees, the berries still without a trace of purple in them, the leaves a teary brown. It's the end of August, the air is full of swallows gathering for the great migration. An army band is rehearsing in the corner, drums and trumpets glint in the sun. They're playing "Die Himmel rühmen" and "Ich schieß den Hirsch im wilden Forst." It's the fifth year of the war, and it's another world, a sort of *béguinage*, everything within is hushed and quiet, the shouted orders don't concern you. A town in the east, above it the high plateau, crowned by our Montsalvat, the buildings and the vast yard pale yellow, the whole thing like a desert fortress. Even the surrounding places are full of oddities. Unmade roads, half on the flat, half on a steep incline; isolated houses that no track leads to, who knows how their inhabitants get home; fences like in Lithuania, low, mossy, damp. A gypsy caravan converted into a dwelling. A man walks along in the evening, a cat perched on his left shoulder; the cat has a piece of string round its neck, cranes out to one side, wants to jump down, the man laughs. Low clouds, black and violet light, dull, louring sky, poplars. In front of a wall, for no obvious horticultural reason, three blue roses trellised in the form of a lyre. The mornings characterized by a particularly soft auroral light. Here too everywhere a sense of unreality, two-dimensional stage sets.

Ringing the exercise hall the dormitory blocks: dreams. Not so much of victory and fame, but dreams of solitude, evanescence, ghostliness. Reality is remote. At the head of the entrance block, the so-called honor hall, the name of a general in big letters: "General von X barracks." A World War I general. For three days I made a point of asking the sentries each time I passed: Who is the barracks named for? Who was General von X? I never got an answer. General von X totally eclipsed. Vanished. Lowered his banner, his car flag, his general staff that danced attendance on him. Obsolete after just two decades. All too palpable here the mortal, the ephemeral, the misestimates, the distortions.

The blocks are flooded periodically by waves of recruits. They are of two types: there are the sixteen-year-olds, undernourished, skinny, poor work-service types, timid, submissive, anxious; and the old guys, in their fifties, from Berlin. On the first day, the latter are still gentlemen, wearing mufti, buying newspapers, walking with a bustle that says: we're lawyers/independent traders/insurance agents, with pretty wives and central heating, these temporary conditions do not concern us, some of them are even waggish—on the second day they're in uniform, and groveling. Now they have to run along the corridors when a sergeant yells, look lively in the yard, lug crates, jam helmets on. The training course is not long: two or three weeks. What's interesting is that rifle practice now begins on day two, earlier it wasn't until after four to six weeks. Then, one night, they muster with pack, rolled-up coat, canvas, gas mask, submachine gun, rifle—almost a hundredweight of baggage—and they march off into the dark to be loaded up. Their departure has something ghostly about it. An unseen band leads them off, playing marches, brisk jolly *tempi*, behind it the silent column stamps into oblivion. The whole thing happens very quickly, a rip in the silence and darkness, then the plateau has reverted to its familiar dark earth- and heavenless night. The following morning the next lot arrive. Who in turn stamp off. The weather has turned cold now for those exercising outside. Commands are given: rub your hands, hit your fists against your knees, stimulate your circulation, life is kept going, military biology. The blocks stay where they are, the waves pass through them. Ever new waves of men, waves of blood, destined to dribble away into the Eastern steppes after a few shots and gestures toward so-called enemies. Unfathomable the whole, were it not for the impressive general, ravishing in his purple and gold, who shoots and gives orders to shoot, his pension isn't even under threat. At twelve noon the officers lunch together in the canteen. There has been no difference in rations between officers and men since the beginning of the war. A colonel and a rifleman get the same two loaves of army bread a week, plus margarine, and artificial honey on paper strips to pick up. Lunch is a bowl of cabbage soup or a few boiled potatoes, which you peel on the table top (oilcloth, if still extant, otherwise someone has "organized" a sheet for the purpose), you put the potatoes to the side, and wait for soup or gravy.

One day the colonel in command of my detachment appears—unshaven. There are no more razor blades, or strops, for that matter. One man claims to know somewhere in Berlin where something of the sort can be organized. An Austrian comrade chips in with the observation that in the Habsburg army only the Windischgrätzer Dragoons went around clean-shaven as of right—a memory of Kolin, where the newly arrived recruits, babyfaces to a man, decided the course of the battle. One piece of shaving soap has to last four months. In the men's barber shop they don't do shaves anymore, for want of wherewithal. In America, meanwhile, they shave lying down—typical of that bunch of pampered plutocrats.

Our conversations are those of nice, harmless people, none of whom can guess what is in store for himself or the Fatherland. Badoglio is a traitor, the king a bastard sawn off by rickets. They've found a sort of ur-fraternity cap in a Holstein funeral tump, proof of the highly developed cap-making skills of our ancestors thirty-five hundred years ago. Did you know the Greeks were Aryans too? Prince Eugen outlived his fame, what he did at the end in France wasn't that great. We don't think much of the newfangled short dagger, the cavalry still wear their long sabers—cavalry! All of them now bicycle brigades—once the name of the rank was Rittmeister (Master of Horse), now it's Radmeister (Master of Bicycles).

All these people, however martial their bearing, are basically thinking only of how they might contrive to smuggle a dish of mushrooms home to the wife when they go on furlough, whether their boy is keeping up at school, and that they mustn't land on the street like in 1918, if—and this is the expression you hear, that they like to use—if things "go pear-shaped." Almost all of them are officers of the old army, aged about fifty or so, veterans of the Great War. In the intervening time, they were reps for cigarette or paper companies, agricultural officials, equerries in riding clubs, they've all muddled along on civvy street. Now they're majors. No one speaks a foreign language, or has visited a foreign country, except in wartime. Only our Austrian cousin, always alert and a little neurotic about being condescended to, has slightly wider horizons, no doubt on account of Austria's old ties to the Adriatic and the Balkans. In the evening they read and discuss Skowronnek: "impressive reach." It promised no great intellectual depth, but I was always alert in this company. There were none of us who weren't preoccupied with the one question, how it had been possible, and was still possible today, that Germany continued to follow this so-called government, this half-dozen shouters, who for ten years now have been replaying the same guff in the same halls to the same rowdy listeners, these six prize idiots who thought they knew it all, better than anyone in centuries heretofore, and than the common sense of the rest of the world. Gamblers who had gone to Monte Carlo to bust the bank with their wretched system; cardsharps, so inept as to assume the other players wouldn't notice the marked cards they were playing with—club-wielding clowns, heroes with brass knuckles. This wasn't the Staufers' dream of linking north and south, nor the at least irreproachably colonialist notion of the Teutonic knights heading east, no, it was the detritus of ambition and form, primal rain-dance stuff, Henry the Lion's nightly torchlight celebrations with a cast of plywood coffins.

That was the regime, plain to see, and now the war is in its fifth year, lying there glumly with defeats and miscalculations, vacated continents, torpedoed battleships, casualties by the million, bombed out metropolises, and the masses are still listening to and believing the Führer's twaddle. There's no mistaking that. At any rate, those living outside the bombed cities believe firmly in the new weapons, secret retribution machines, dependable and imminent counterblows. High and low, general and kitchen orderly alike. A mystical totality of fools, a babbling collective of unteachables—something terribly German about it, and only to be explained in that ethnological way. Two peripheral ethnological explanations suggest themselves, firstly that the middle-sized towns and the countryside have little direct experience of the war, they are given enough to eat, and can organize the rest; they haven't sat through bombing raids; emotionally, Goebbels keeps them supplied in house and sty; and in the countryside the weather always mattered more than ideas anyway. Second, family losses are accommodated far more easily than the nation would have you think. The dead die quickly, and the more people die, the quicker they are forgotten. Between father and son there is probably just as much antipathy as its opposite; hate holds them in suspension just as much as love binds them together. Yes, dead sons are useful to a career, they bring tax reductions, and make old age more important. It would be a good and useful thing if young people were taught that; it would enable them to draw their own conclusions later on, when they were told about the immortality of heroes and the gratitude of the survivors.

In detail the picture looked like this: in the fifth year of the war, the army was kept going by just two ranks, its lieutenants and its field marshals, nothing else matters. The lieutenants, products of the Hitler Youth, therefore fitted out with a training that was by its nature a systematic eradication of all moral and intellectual perspectives from literature and life, and their re-placement by Gothic chieftains and dirks—and hay barns to sleep in on exercises. Kept safe from any educated, old-school parents, teachers, priests, or other humanist influences, or cul-tured people of any type, and this already in peacetime: con-scious, purposive, and well drilled, they were perfectly equipped to undertake the destruction of the continent as their Aryan assignment. And on the field marshals, just a word: it's a little-known fact that they receive their field marshal's salary, un-taxed, for the rest of their lives, and also get a staff officer as adjutant for keeps, and when they leave active service, they re-ceive an estate or nicely dimensioned piece of land in Grune-wald. Since, under our constitution, the same one man giveth and taketh away the rank of marshal, and in this latter capacity he has taken away titles, medals, and pensions, and promulgated the collective liability of kith and kin, a field marshal ends up looking something like a paterfamilias. In any case, they were hardly anyone's idea of devils.

If you reflect on the war and the preceding peace, there's one thing you mustn't leave out of account: namely, the quite ex-traordinary existential vacuum of the German man of today who was given none of the things that routinely fill up the inner space of other peoples: proper national contents, an alert citizenry, political debate, social life, colonial impressions, authentic historical facts—what we had here was a vacuum of pseudo-historical bilge, suppressed culture, shamelessly stupid government lies, and cheap sports. But to go around in an eye-catching uniform, to receive salutes and lean across maps, to clack through halls and across yards with a retinue—to issue commands, conduct inspections, and talk bombastically ("I don't repeat orders"; the subject was cleaning a toilet), all that engenders a feeling of occupying space, of individual expansion, multiplied effectiveness, in a word, that complex that the average individual craves. With art forbidden, newspapers driven out of business, and personal dissent answered by a shot in the neck—to apply human and ethical measures to the filling up of space, the way the cultured peoples did, well, all that wasn't possible in the Third Reich. What obtained here was a pretend space; when he was put to sprinting across pontoon bridges moments before they were blown up, under the eyes of telescopic sights, the individualist felt like a one-man cosmic catastrophe.

The supreme command of the Wehrmacht has a press section responsible for morale and fighting spirit. Led, how could it be otherwise, by a general. Staffed by numerous writers from Weimar and the Nazi epoch. I pay close attention to its productions, "Bulletins to the Troops," "Bulletins to the Officer Corps," "Material for Schools," "How to Address a Company," and so on and so forth. All this is of course publicly available. Stylistically, this section is part of Goebbels's ministry, and is specialized in soldiers' vocabulary: douchebag, cunt, piece of shit—that's the intellectual level, and is applied to anyone who might think differently. There are regular references to the "young nations" who would claim victory as their birthright. Young nation, indeed! Even the supreme command will have heard of Julius Caesar, who was murdered in 44 B.C.—well, even in his day this young nation managed to make quite a nuisance of itself. Unless all nations are the same age, Russia must be twenty-seven next birthday, so, to go by the Nazi hypothesis, it must be marked down for victory. The Japanese emerged from their legends at 660 B.C., they are as old as the hills, their Shinto religion disappears into the dim and distant. The USA came into being, racially and as a state, during the seventeenth century, just at the time baroque was declining in Italy and Leibniz in Germany was developing his historical philosophy. So all those appeals to vital young nations are just so much guff, predicated on the officially sanctioned disappearance of German education. The morale unit describes what it does as "a kingly art" that "speaks to the noblest and proudest character traits of the German," even the salute was to be the "expression of respect to the idea of a fighting Germany" and so on. Other tropes include: "The triumph of arms to be followed by a triumph of cradles!" The Nuremberg Laws are instituted "not just to protect German blood, but also German honor"; and then there is the "deadly peril" in which we have found ourselves, and "the Führer's promised rescue in the eleventh hour." These bulwarks alone enable the soldier in captivity to break the "intellectual terror" of the enemy. Of course the Jewish-Bolshevik press must be wiped out; it was especially important (in December 1943) for the soldiers to be made to understand ("as simply as possible, and as vividly as possible") "that Stalin has suffered a great political defeat in the last ten years." Further stock-in-trade includes: *Italy*: traitors, shameless comportment, sons of bitches; the *Russians*: out for revenge, sadistic perverts, hate-filled steppes; the *Americans* steal watches, wallets, and fountain pens from the wounded. Stalin, the lizard, the gangster from Tbilisi; Roosevelt, the outlaw in chief, driving Ecuador and Bolivia into the war at the point of his six-shooter; Churchill, the whisky drinker, who as a stripling threw over a middle-class English girl for the sake of an American heiress. Above all, never lower your guard: political jokes—report them; bar girls—all suspect; listeners to foreign radio stations, traitors—shot in the neck.

But there is another way as well, arguably less shrill, which employs Hölderlin and Rilke. It's interesting to trace the way those two poets were used in the propaganda of recent years. "*Dir ist, Liebes, keiner zuviel gefallen*" ("not one too manuy, my dear, has fallen for you") is the most widely used quotation from the one, with "*auch hier sind Götter*" ("here too are gods") applied to wished-for coups. While with Rilke, the introduction of a Cornet into his world of paupers, monks, and pale duchesses is enough to let the mildness and devotion of the other work appear in a more favorable light. Listen: in the *Naval Review* of November 1943 (published by Mittler & Son; the editor, inevitably, is an admiral) that makes its way through our blocks, a professor for church and international law at a Bavarian university treats questions of war at sea (a *church* lawyer?) under four aspects, "military, economic, political, and moral-intellectual." On the first head: "A lasting gain is the possibility of easy access to the Atlantic, and thereby the guarantee of flourishing trade and cultural life, for us, and for all Europe. As Hölderlin put it: '*Es beginnet nämlich der Reichtum im Meere*' ['for wealth is born in the sea']." And on the last: "The new creed is the primacy of experience. Some readers may be aware that even before the scientists, a poet in his own way prepared the ground for this innovation: Rainer Maria Rilke in his *Duino Elegies*." Note the qualification "in his own way," i.e., to the best of his ability, he's just a poet, and science of course does these things better. On the nature of the "experience" in this new "creed" not a word. Now, it's possible to come at the *Duino Elegies* from many angles, but to interpret them as in some sense *warlike* is something they really won't bear. The allusion to Rilke is a trap for what the professor correctly assumes is the enfeebled German brain.

The autumn around the blocks was, as it was the length and breadth of the Reich, parlously dry, the fields are overrun by mice, the potato harvest is catastrophic, the beets don't contain enough sugar. The loss of territories to the east signifies, in food terms, the loss of two months of bread, and one of fat and one of meat. Rations are cut. There are no top boots anymore, leather is in short supply; there are no more artificial limbs for casualties, the material is used up. There are no more shoelaces or false teeth, no material for bandages, and no sample bottles for urine; doctors are few and far between, entire divisions go into battle without a single field surgeon, in parts the civilian population has one doctor per twenty-five thousand patients, and she has no petrol. But the Führer doles out badges, he has ideas about the width of ribbons for wreaths at army funerals, he forbids the soldiers to intermarry with foreign women, not even Scandinavians: "the noblest Nordic woman" remains "racial flotsam" compared to our Greater Germans. Every pore sweats rot, but—or therefore—the propaganda goes full pelt. We open our illustrated magazines: Nera and Sehra, the "little imps of Mostar" are thrilled to participate in the great Organization Todt; Goebbels dazzles the wounded with his white teeth; Göring puts in an appearance as Santa Claus—the fairy tale engrosses us.

One November day I am required to go to Berlin for work. It's a time when travel is among the most arduous forms of competitive sport. There is no regular train service anymore. At two in the morning at the station I leave from, a miracle train draws up: eight *wagons-lits*, four first- and four second-class carriages, hardly anyone on it, at the back a carriage with an ack-ack crew. I get on. An SS man pulls me off right away. I don't understand it. He tells me it's the train from Führer HQ and is strictly reserved for top brass. I can see that my briefcase might well contain the odd hand grenade. I board the next train, or rather, I squeeze into the third-class lavatory in my colonel's uniform, among laborers from the East. The lavatory is open to all, women and children have to use it, it's not possible to shut the door, you can't budge, no one bats an eyelid. I have to change trains. On the next one, I get into a second-class carriage, where I have to stand. Three pricks in Party uniform, strong and healthy young men, sprawl over the upholstery. Old white-haired women, others with children, stand in the corridor with me. The master race produces a bottle of cognac and a few bundles of cigars (the mass of the population gets one cigar per day, and no cognac) and for three hours to Berlin strengthens itself for the coming Party tasks. On the same day, all the newspapers carried articles proclaiming that casualties and decorated heroes were disproportionately drawn from the ranks of the Party as against the common people. There were no exemptions made for anyone at all. One encountered the sentence: "Optical impressions to the contrary, occasionally met with, are entirely misleading." Evidently my three fellow travelers were part of such an optical impression.

From Block II, I understood the fog and sniffles of German mythology: the mists and vapors and the constant recourse to bearskin—of "the splendid old Germans," as the radio liked to refer to them; Taine would geophysically infer the primary national aversion to clarity and form, and one might add, candor. In December 1943, at a time when the Russians had pushed us back a thousand miles, and punched holes in our front in a dozen places, a lieutenant colonel, delicate as a hummingbird, mild as a pet rabbit, said to us over lunch: "So long as the bastards don't break through." Break through, mop up, take out, mobile front—the force of those words, positively to dazzle, and negatively to mask a state of affairs. Stalingrad: a tragic accident; the loss of the U-boats: a chance technical discovery on the part of the British; the fact that Montgomery chased Rommel two and a half thousand miles from El Alamein to Naples: betrayal by the Badoglio clique.—At the same time a Party bigwig has occasion to be here, and appears at our table. My colonel, old school, cavalry, Knight of St. John, a man who jumps fences in his monocle, even goes to sleep with it on, now took it off for a pair of black horn-rims, so as not to upset the high-up, or risk his own future ("without fear or favor" "Semper Talis"—the words on the badge of the old Prussian guard).

I have time to read. By chance a French book came into my

hands, about Bernini's stay in Paris in 1665, where he was to design the new Louvre. That seventeenth century! Those French! Bernini reports: Archimedes tells the king, when he wants to reward him for burning the enemy navy, "Give your gold to the gods, because they gave men the circle, and the compasses with which to draw it." He goes on to say, "Such monumental pieces need to be composed in mass, *alle macchie*, as when one cuts out shapes and arranges them in groups without having any single idea in mind, but purely so as to balance the composition. Then you carefully fill in some of the spaces with fill-in shapes, and gradually go down to the level of ornament. That is the only way of making a composition in a great and considered way. There is no other way, otherwise the individual detail—that part that matters least—is too assertive." Somewhere there are people still capable of thinking! These are calmatives, arising out of historic laws, the most influential, so far as we may see.

By now, Christmas is approaching. There are an extra hundred grams of wurst, in addition to the weekly meat ration, which is already 25 percent reconstituted vegetables. Also, anyone who cares to give up thirty grams of margarine and a hundred grams of sugar can order a stollen. I put my name down on the list. Christmas carols are banned, winter equinoctial contemplations professionally solicited, with an emphasis on the return of light from the bosom of Mother Nature, the commanding officers are to give appropriate instructions. There's precious little sign of said return. I stand at the window of Room 66, the barracks yard is in a gray soupy light the gray of gulls' wings that have been dipped in every sea. The festival dawns. That morning there was a great attack on Berlin; you ask yourself whether your apartment house is still standing, and which of your few remaining acquaintances in the city may have survived. Then it's evening, the food is brought in. I ask the orderly how his asthma is, he is hard of hearing, it's difficult to get through to him. I look out across the yard, down to the valley, the steppe, the East—all of it so near, so present, all those grisly beings who understood nothing about themselves. And then it darkens, the Holy Night of the year 1943.

Soon after Christmas, there was the order to vacate the blocks, the defeated troops flooding back from the East wanted the use of them; we move out, myself too. Active, passive—the louse in the fur, the wolf in sheep's clothing, Billy Goat Gruff tending the green shoots: Do they participate, are they principals? What a pompous notion it is: to act, to do! To stand under duress and be dependent on subsidies—it may be to act, but to insist on the identity of action and thought—what a backwoods notion! Imagine a modern physicist wanting to express his calculations, his profession, in his life, to "live by them," or Bachofen his theory of the matriarchy, or Böcklin his *Isle of the Dead*—what a farce! If someone is compelled by events to live in the historical world, among sharpshooters and spivs, trappers and coney catchers, should that cause him to step outside of himself and vigorously express his ideas?

Is there a single idea of mankind anyway? There were probably times when one was present to people's awareness. But opinions today proliferate like migraine attacks—a hereditary evil. A man could have the views of a prophet, and wouldn't have to raise the green flag and move into the highlands with eagle and snake. That prophetic views don't change people, improve them, give them an orientation, is demonstrated by the failure of our latest Dionysus. The blond beast went crazy. Opinions, as a lubricant, to bring movement to the peristalsis of the world—what serious man would step forward with opinions today? Historical world—grown impertinent, and quickly gulped down, in the circle the fatties sit with their concubines and their favorites, and in front of the murderers, the violins play merry tunes, but in the dark the nameless victims are garrotted—no, there's nothing here to step forward for, and nothing to fight, not with the little sling, nor with the big trombone: let them run their thresher over the corn.

The part that lives is not the same as the part that thinks, that's a fundamental fact of our existence, and we had better get used to it. Maybe it used to be different once, maybe in some unguessable future a sidereal union will shimmer along, but for the moment this is how things are. My brain moved in its own space; what lived in me within the constraints of the given milieu was cooperative, polite, and comradely. Thought was without falsehood, it asked no one, it kept itself to itself, it was relaxed, could afford to be, so certain was it that it was right, and had the truth vis-à-vis all the facts of life in the barracks we lived in together. "He that believeth shall not hasten!" proclaims Isaiah. Of course it's tempting to say the faith must be made known; who thinks like that, who sees things as described above, must intervene, take a hand, make a revolution or get himself shot. I don't agree. There is no generally valid proof, there are only existential reasons. With me, these reasons are to be found in my personal unbelief in the significance of the historical world. I haven't managed to make any more of myself than an experimenter who fuses contents and subject-complexes to closed forms, who is capable of appreciating the union of life and mind only in a secondary product: statue, poem, survivable form—I address life, and complete a poem. Everything else that concerns life is questionable and uncertain; we feel no actual connection to the numinous, not to mention the so-called national; the only actual thing is what is grounded in an expressive aesthetic work. Biological tension culminates in art. Art has no historical foundations, it suspends time and history, its effect is on the genes, the inner heredity, the substance—it takes the long, inner route. A few novels may be comic and political, but that's misleading; the nature of art is infinite restraint; its nucleus is smashing, but its periphery is narrow; it touches little, but what it does touch burns. Existential reasons are not causal reasons, they are constitutional, compel no one, apply only to the one to whom they are given as facts; perhaps they are variants, recessive or dominant strains, or, as above: experiments. They are not communicable or examinable, they seek their legitimation in the necessity of the world of expression, not shrinking from wandering around these blocks too, yes, perhaps even seeing in the blocks a particular challenge to consult their own foundations.

The blocks will reject the association out of hand. What speaks like that, the blocks will reply, is thought, cold, unfruitful thought that threatens warm and natural life, the intellect gone feral, alien to patriotic impulses, the idea of empire, of harvest festivals, and *Snow White and the Seven Dwarfs*. Only today, in the higher-brow of our newspapers, we saw a photograph headed "Artistic Creation on the Front" with the subtitle: "The Commander gives an adjutant his opinion of the photograph

'Enemy Steam'"—so? The commander eh, another admiral no doubt—and the storm lashes the waves and the lighter or freighter and the minelayer or minesweeper stamp or steam, and there's any amount of spray sloshing around too (friendly steam / enemy steam) the whole pathetic victory mania—indeed. Compared to that my own idea is implacable—enemy steam / friendly steam, *qu'importe*, it's my primary humanity, everything else is criminal!

Now the idea in turn has had the idea that something has come into the world to relieve the absolute, love, and that the mild one was sent to move the idea, to bow down voluntarily—as I say, but love, and not stubbornness. Where love and the idea interplay there will always be the lofty world which man will also struggle to express. But the idea has only this age, it is working on the measure of all things, expression, features, mouth; with that its terrestrial calling ends.

One is supposed to extend one's love to criminals, but probably not all of them. It came to Rodya when he took Sonia and suffered, Rodion Raskolnikov, who first dared everything to spit in everyone's faces, to take all power to himself, even dared murder—it came to him when Sonia said: Come with me now, stop at the crossroads, kiss the earth you foul, before whom you have sinned, then bow down to the whole world and say aloud: I am the murderer. Will you do that? Will you come?—And he came.

And then the end came in the East. If you had gone to the Town Commandant on January 27, 1945, and asked him what should be done with all the things we had lugged out here from Berlin when the Russians come, the adjutant, an SS captain, would have replied: Anyone who asks a question like that will be put up against the wall, the Russians won't get through, maybe the odd tank patrol can be seen in the distance, but the town will be defended, and anyone who sends his wife back to Berlin, for instance, will be shot. Then at 5 a.m. we heard the alarm, artillery attack, and we slogged home through the blizzard, with a briefcase, at 10 below, along the icy avenues choked with endless columns of refugees with covered wagons, spilling dead children on the ground. In Küstrin we were put on an open cattle car that took twelve hours to get us the forty miles to Berlin-Zoo, under air attack. That was more or less how the war ended, up and down the Eastern front, in town after town. There were strangers in our apartment, the rooms were picked bare, we covered ourselves with my soldier's coat and newspapers only to wake up to the shrill of sirens. That was the end of block life and Room 66.

In those barracks I wrote the *Novel of the Phenotype*, many parts of *World of Expression*, including "Pallas," and some of the *Static Poems*, among them, "Ah, the Faraway Land—," "September," "Then—," "Static Poems," and others.

# LETTER FROM BERLIN, JULY 1948

*To the editor of a literary monthly in southern Germany*

... allow me to reply as follows to your invitation to contribute to the *Merkur*: I am in the rather unusual situation of having been banned since 1936, excluded from literature then, and still and again on the list of undesirables today. Given these circumstances, I cannot think it would be a good idea for me to go back into print with some quodlibetical piece or other, something that might sit well in the context of an established journal and the taste of an editor licensed within certain intellectual limits. Rather, I would like to be able to determine the extent and type of work myself, exactly, and see that it represents my new thinking ...

Because in the past years I have written several books which have taken me forward to new experiences, but which would not seem agreeable in the context of German literary and cultural business. I am happy to report, therefore, that a poetry book of mine will appear this summer with a Swiss firm, and the—probably more impressive—prose works possibly as well, in a neutral setting, far from the current German confusions. Lest you jump to any false conclusions, let me add that my questionnaire,* to which you referred, is all in order, as countless checks

* This is the "*Fragebogen*" that the Office of Military Government, United States— which administered the area of Germany controlled by the U.S. Army after World

and investigations within my medical sphere have confirmed. I never belonged to the Party, nor to any of its bodies; I have nothing to fear from the law at any point—which only makes the arguments of those who will not have me back in literature the more frantic.

I don't know where such people are drawn from, politically, and I have taken no steps to get in touch with them. Fame has no white wings, Balzac says; but if you have been called a swine by the Nazis, an idiot by the Communists, an intellectual prostitute by the Democrats, a renegade by the emigrants, and a pathological nihilist by the devout (as I have, and all in the last fifteen years), it does rather take the edge off a man's appetite for the public intellectual life. All the more so, if one feels no particular connection to that life anyway. I for my part have followed the literary production of the last three years, and my sense of it is as follows: for the past four decades now in the West the same group of heads has been talking about the same set of problems with the same set of arguments using the same set of causal and conditional sentences, and come to the same set of conclusions, which they are pleased to call a synthesis, albeit of nonresults, or more simply a crisis—the whole thing is *vieux jeu*, an old libretto, stiff and scholastic, a typology put together from stage set and dust. A people—or indeed the West as a whole—wanting to renew itself, and there are suggestions that

---

War II—distributed to those Germans it thought might be Nazis. Where there was nothing to say, or nothing was said, this was derisorily referred to as a "*Persilschein*," a "clean note." In 1951, the author Ernst von Salomon published a very widely read novel called *Der Fragebogen*.

it might be capable of doing so, will not be renewed by such methods.

The only way a people will regenerate itself is by an emanation of spontaneous elements, not by the cultivation and grafting of historicizing and descriptive ones. And yet it is these last that fill our public space. And as the background to this process I see something that, if I say it, you will certainly find catastrophic. The West is not declining because of totalitarian systems or SS crimes, nor yet by its material impoverishment or by the various Gottwalds and Molotovs, but by the craven crawling of its intelligentsia to political concepts. The *zoon politikon*, that Greek infelicity, that Balkan idea—that is at the heart of the decline we are now passing into. That their political ideas are the crucial, primary ones, has not been questioned by that intelligentsia of the clubs and meetings for a long time now; rather, they try to wag their tails at them, and come over as supportable in the context of them. This is true not only of Germany, which in this regard is in a particularly difficult, almost forgivable situation, but for all the other European intelligences, with the possible exception of England, from where one hears occasionally a different sort of noise.

If we cast a brief look at these political concepts and what they contain in the way of degenerative and regenerative substance—for example, Democracy, the best sort of basis for a state, but absurd as a productive element! Expression comes not from majority decisions, but more like the opposite, the distancing of oneself from such results, it is produced by an act of will in isolation. Or the humanities, a thing the public likes to endow with a positive halo—of course one should be human—but there were high cultures, among them some very near to our own, which utterly failed to act on this precept, such as Egypt, Greece, and [Olmec, Mayan] Yucatán. Its secondary character in the area of productivity, its anti-regenerative strain is evident. Everything primary is explosive, later followed by finessing and smoothing—one of the few indisputable insights of modern genetics. Entelechy mutates spasmodically, not historically. That is a general law. But wherever there is a suggestion of something primary in our intellectual life, some volcanic element, it is attacked and destroyed in our pasteurizing media; to wit, those individuals described above appear with their debating clubs, their roundtable meetings, their assembly matadors, and they issue appeals, collect signatures in the name of past and future, of history, of our grandchildren, of mothers and children; the cultural philosophers, the cultural interpreters, the crisis phenomenologists stream out, and denounce, eliminate, exterminate— and of course also Messrs. editors in their big press limousines as the professional dam-patchers, unfortunately, usually, before time—and everything to the protection of democracy and humanity. What use is all this talk about the West and renewal and crisis if the only thing that can be renewed is what exists anyway, useful enough in its limited context, but as a principle of regeneration, in times of change or beginning, capable of bringing forth only slack and atrophied forms?

The situation is regrettable, because there are new elements around, and the West might be able to risk a new start. There is no question for me but that a cerebral mutation is in process, held down by everything called the public under the leadership of the state-organized eradication of all being. And here begins the tragedy: the consensus is right, the consensus is historically always right. Because the elements point to a being that has destructive traits (and those are always alarming), new traits of the depigmented quaternary—man is not what preceding centuries thought and assumed, and in his new thought structure he will send the Western idea of history to the same junk heap as the cult of Wotan or the sacrifice of the shaman.

It is not my profession to confront the public with these tragic thoughts of my own. I think them by and for myself; one of their conditions being that a man, breaching his own frontiers and going out before the generality, unasked, unexistential and peripheral, appears before time. I bear the objections to them alone too: estheticism, isolationism, esotericism—"the intellectual crane-flight over the heads of the people"—yes, I am if you like an ornithologist specializing in those cranes, which harm no one, to which all can look up, or follow with their eyes, and invest with their dreams. They are directed against a sort of animal monism, that everything must fit together, everything be supplied for everyone else free of charge, without difficulty, without adversity, without the experience of defeat, without the posture-forming resignation. And then they point toward a process that seems to me imminent: the coming century will take the world of man and confront him with a decision, with no emigration and no way out; there will be only two types, two constitutions, two reactions: those who act and are ambitious, and those who silently await transformation, the history makers and the profound; the criminals and the monks—and I'm on the side of the surplices.

And with that I conclude my letter, for whose length and

manner I apologize. You offered me a friendly wave with your glove, and I reply with something approaching a horsewhip. But I repeat: I am not extrapolating, I am not spreading my own existence beyond my constitution. You should take from these lines only that I am not greatly concerned about not appearing in print—if my name appears in my lifetime, then good; if not, also good; if something is printed after my death, very well, if not, ditto—my nihilism is universal, it is supportive, it knows the unthinkable transformation.

And with that, farewell, and greetings from a blockaded, blacked-out Berlin, from that part of it that as a consequence of that Greek mistake and the world it led to is presently busy starving. Written in a shady room, in which maybe two hours of twenty-four have had light, for a gloomy rainy summer further robs the city of all chance of a brief happiness, and since spring has mantled its ruins with fall. But it is the city whose brilliance I loved, and whose misery I now accept as home, where I lived in the Second, Third, and now Fourth Reich, and which nothing will cause me to leave. Yes, one could even predict a future for it: there will be tensions in its sobriety, difference and interferences in its clarity, something ambiguous will set in, an ambivalence from which centaurs or amphibious creatures will be born. Let us finally thank General Clay, and hope that his Skymasters carry this letter safely to you.

# KNUT HAMSUN:
## ON OVERGROWN PATHS 1949

This book is as silly-sweet as many of his books are; it is at once good-natured and cynical. One shouldn't take any of his sentences completely seriously; he himself patently doesn't take them seriously either. He reminds me of a big old lion, blinking contemptuously from his cage at the zoo visitors, and, when he thinks he sees a lawyer or doctor among them, spitting in their direction through the bars.

*Pan*, *Mysteries*, and *Hunger* moved us deeply, and ripped clear the last traces of respect for civilization from our bodies. The novels of his middle period, the great epic period, like *Segelfoss Town*, showed us his substance and methods still more clearly: an overwhelming abundance of human figures—I suppose one has to call them human figures, but one might as well say beetles and mites in human form—he picks them up for a moment, turns them over, looks at them from in front and behind, and then sets them back down, both humanely and with vast indifference, and goes on his way. When Thomas Mann called him "the greatest living writer," we agreed without a murmur.

Then something political happened—what it was in detail is neither to be ascertained from this book nor from documents available in Germany—and now people come along and say, this man is shameless and dangerous, and we want nothing to do with him. He pays no regard to what we went through politically, and what we won't allow to be taken from us because it has been the most of our lives; without it, we would be left with nothing at all, nothing to show and nothing to go on with, we wouldn't be at all as significant as we would like to be, and not as tragic as we want to appear—so away with him.

It's an interesting point of view, because it presents us with a fundamental decision. The point of view shows us the great schism that cuts through the Western world: on the one hand there is art and all to do with it, and on the other there is good, warm, uninterrupted family life, propped on insurance policies, pensions, "claims" to this and that for the rest of our days, underwritten and tempered by a kind of beer-warmer, which is the state. The latter too is a point of view that has much to be said for it, and is perfectly defensible, so long as it is expressed truthfully and with consequence. But to declare on the one hand that we want art, and on the other that we like our welfare state, because only those who live in welfare live pleasantly*—that is not honest, and in the long run not viable. Art is more precious than the humdrum perks of someone's existence, and making art, anthropologically speaking, is more in keeping with our species than the handful railing against it because their personal lives did not turn out as expected.

* Quoted, a little mischievously, from Bertolt Brecht's "Ballade vom angenehmen Leben" ("Ballad of the Pleasant Life") in act 2 of the *Dreigroschenoper* (*The Three-penny Opera*) of 1928. The socially engaged poet and playwright wrote about practical and political and ethical problems; the "tragic" poet and doctor kept literature and any philanthropic feelings he may have had rigidly separate.

A trouble-free and purposeful art—of course no one would actually call it that, they would mythologize it, and call it contemptuously: Pan. But Pan is silent, at the most he would take out his flute and blow some new reed song—he won't even prick up his ears, and that will drive them to fury and beyond. Now Kant is called in, and his Königsberg dream, and suddenly the moral law is without breach and crisis—but the latitudes and geography and the changing cultural circles leave certain questions open. Then along comes "the wheel of history" which is supposed to drive art—but art is supposed to be deathless and timeless as well, and collective—what a mess! So finally, it's force majeure and legal precedent and "the highest judges in the land have sentenced him."—But as we've seen, there are judges and judges. In a word: a textbook case. What the political man is incapable of seeing is solitude, asceticism, monasticism—art. But if humanity didn't have those things, it wouldn't be human. And on the other hand, there are certain other things it can well do without, and has often done without, certain shining civilizational attainments. Among them, perhaps such things as vengeance dressed up as censorship, or personal resentment as critical discrimination.

## I NEVER HAD DIFFERENCES . . . 1952

I never had differences with any of my publishers, never expected or accepted advances from any of them. Publishers are not by their nature patrons, but enlightened merchant-princes. I am grateful to all of mine, and to the booksellers who put my difficult books on display.

## "DO YOU WRITE AT A DESK?" 1952

An old desk is at the heart of my enterprise. Picture it to your-selves, if you will, like this: my medical practice and my writing share one room. My desk (73 × 135 cm) is covered with stacks of correspondence (which I don't answer), manuscripts sent to me (which I haven't yet gotten around to reading), magazines, books, samples of medicines, rubber stamps (for prescriptions), three biros, two ashtrays, a telephone. There isn't really any space for writing, but I clear myself some with my elbow. This is where I scrawl with my bad doctor's handwriting, which I can't read myself, until I've reached a stage when I can go on to the typewriter, which is on the microscope table.

My room is on the ground floor, and faces the yard and the back. The view takes in a rabbit run with a white rabbit in it (it belongs to the janitor's wife), some clotheslines, usually full, then some hydrangeas I have often written about, which stay in flower until November, and ends at the rear walls of the houses opposite, which are gray, crumbly, and dilapidated. It is a room and a desk from which cultured visitors have been known to re-coil in dismay.

This and that and the other thing have been developed here since 1945. I should say, the intellectual groundwork for them has been laid at a third table the night before: namely in my local pub (two hours), where I sit at my regular place, read, think, listen to the radio, peruse the letters from the three people with whom I am in contact.

Three desks in all, then, or tables. The decisive one is the one with the typewriter on it, because only type invites judgment, presents an objective face, the surface reflecting the imaginative to the critical self. All are somewhat cluttered—not long ago I was standing outside an antique shop, and my eye lit on a desk, 2 by 3 meters, with gleaming, almost black varnish, perfectly empty—from where, I told myself, something a little more expansive could surely have been produced.

## "WHAT MAY READERS LOOK FORWARD TO?" 1953

At present I am not working on anything, except the gathering of new impressions, and testing of the methods and principles I have previously followed.

# AGING AS A PROBLEM
# FOR ARTISTS 1954

It's possible I may have bitten off a little more than I can chew
with this subject. In case you feel inclined to tell me so when I
finish, kindly bear in mind that, to the best of my knowledge, it
has rarely been isolated as it is here, that the literature on it is
very slight, and that I have had to flesh it out with my own ex-
perience and understanding.

An array of factors, inner and outer, brought me to the sub-
ject. Last winter in Berlin I attended a talk at the Kant Society,
where an expert was talking about the so-called *Opus postumum*
of Kant, the originals of which disappeared in northern Ger-
many during World War II, but of which copies made over the
past two decades have survived, with comments and textual
notes that had been made available to philosophical circles, al-
beit not completed. This *Opus postumum* was written between
1797 and 1803, some twenty years after the great early work of
Kant. It now transpired that in this posthumous work, some of
his positions were reversed, there were objections to the *Critique
of Pure Reason*, and the speaker broached the question of which
had the greater validity, the early or the posthumous writings,
they were hardly compatible. He did not answer his own ques-
tion, but gave a sense that on occasion the later theses overturned
the earlier. This gave rise to the question of the relation between

early and late work, of the continuity of the productive self, its discontinuities and changes. Our man was talking about philosophy, but one encounters the same problem in the arts.

At about the same time, I was reading a newspaper review of an exhibition of the work of Lorenzo Lotto held the summer before in Venice. The review contained the sentence "In the works of the last decades, the onlooker may feel a manifest hesitancy, as with the German painters Baldung Grien and Cranach." So all these luminaries apparently became uncertain in the work of their latter years. While I was thinking about this, in another work of art history I came upon the following pronouncement from the artist Edward Burne-Jones: "Our first fifty years are passed in grave errors, and then we become timid, barely capable of setting one foot before the other, so well do we know our own weakness. Then there follow twenty years full of effort, and now we begin to understand what we are capable of, and what we must leave undone. And then there comes a ray of hope and a burst of trumpets, and it is time for us to quit this earth." So this was the opposite case to Lotto, here it is youth that is unsure, and old age that is certain, when it is too late. It recalls a scene in *The Death of Titian* written by the twenty-year-old Hugo von Hofmannsthal: Titian is dying, but is painting one last picture, I think a Danae, when suddenly he leaves off, and sends for his early paintings: "He says he has to see them, / the old, the pitiful, the pallid, / to compare them to the new work he is painting now, / certain difficult issues are now clear to him, / he has a terrible sense / of what a sorry dauber he was up till now." Here too, from the artist himself, the former and the current: only in his ninety-first year does he cease to be a sorry dauber.

To my surprise I encountered similar trains of thought when I looked east. In Hokusai (1760–1849) I found the following: "From the age of six, I was mad keen on drawing. By the time I was fifty, I had published a great many drawings, but everything I did before my seventy-third year is worthless. Approaching the age of seventy-three, I began to understand something of the true nature of animals, plants, fishes, and insects. By the time I am eighty, I shall have progressed further, with ninety I will be able to see through to the secret nature of things, and when I am a hundred and ten, everything of mine, be it no more than a line or a dot, will be full of life." Here the question—familiar also in the context of literature—is begged: What would have become of this or that person, if he had died earlier, in his case therefore, what would have survived of Hokusai if he had died before his seventy-third birthday?

Both Eastern and Western lands rest in the peace of his hands—and so I sought counsel from our Olympian forefather and took down his *Maxims and Reflections*, a book that anyone with worries should read in for a few hours each week. There I found the following aphorisms:

1. Growing old is effectively to begin a new business, all circumstances are changed, and one needs either to stop acting altogether or else to take on the new role with understanding and determination.
2. The old man needs to do more than the young man.
3. Mme. Roland facing the guillotine called for writing materials to note down the special thoughts she was sure to have. A pity they were refused her: because at life's end the

braced spirit will think things not previously thought, they will be like happy devils settling on the gleaming mountaintops of the past.

Happy devils—on the way to the scaffold! Very Olympian, very gigantic, and that great-grandfather of ours certainly had enough about him to start a new business at any time, but it probably wasn't universally applicable. But the same volume contains the fragment "Pandora," and I made the acquaintance of that strange character Epimetheus: "My parents called me Epimetheus, / that I might mull over things past, go over hasty events / more slowly to myself, by taking thought / visit the blurred realm of shape-changing possibility." Mulling over, going over, taking thought, the blurred realm of mixing things that were and the might-have-been—surely Epimetheus is the patron saint of old age, twilit, blurred, facing the past, the torch already lowered in his hand.

At this point I can hear you saying to yourselves, our speaker is assembling lots of quotations, he has his ear to the ground in all sorts of places, he is going in search of advice like a young girl traveling alone, but what is really going on here—is there some personal motive involved? You're right, there is, there is some personal motive as well, but it won't take up too much space in what follows. But think for a moment, if you will, an author with a dramatic past, living in dramatic times, emerging among a group of cogenerationists from many countries who underwent broadly the same stylistic evolution, call it futurism, expressionism, surrealism, which even today enlivens the discussion, a stylistic revolution really—though, admittedly, in the view of our author, no more revolutionary than previous styles like impressionism or the baroque or mannerism. Still, at least in the context of this century, it was revolutionary. Our author has followed various pursuits: he was a poet and an essayist, a citizen and a soldier, a settler moved in from the country-side, and an *homme du monde* in some of the great cities of the world—usually controversial, usually opposed, our author has reached a certain age, and is still publishing. If he has not entirely quelled the volcanic element in him, if he has not entirely lost the élan of youth, the critics today say: "My God, won't the man leave us in peace at last, couldn't he write something classical, and if possible Christian? Can't he be a little mature and considered, as becomes his gray hairs?" And then when this author does happen to write something mild and dispassionate, and (inasmuch as it is in his gift to do so) classical, then they say: "He's gone completely senile. He was interesting when he was young, when he had his Sturm und Drang time, but today he's like a copy of himself. What has he got to say to us; why couldn't he have the decency to shut up?"

All well and good. If a book by an author is reviewed, favorably or otherwise, he can be pleased or annoyed accordingly. But the situation is different when the author is so advanced in years, has become so ancient, that whole books have been published about him, essays and theses with which the next generation are earning degrees and doctorates, at home and abroad, in which he is analyzed, systematized, catalogued, in which a comma he placed thirty years previously, or a diphthong he drew out to its full length one Sunday afternoon after the Great War, are treated as fundamental style issues. Interesting studies, supersubtle linguistic and stylistic analyses, but to our author it feels like vivisection being practiced on him; he is known and now he comes to know himself for the first time, thus far he was wholly obscure, he had to reach his age in order to know himself.

If it further happens that this author at some time in his life has expressed views which are later reckoned to be "inappropriate"; these views are now trailed in his wake, and people are happy when, like a horse drawing a harrow across a field, the harrow keeps clipping his heels. Well, our author says to himself, that's just the way things are, that can't be helped. If one only wrote what it would be opportune to have written fifteen years later, then presumably one wouldn't write anything at all. A short instance of this, and then we'll say goodbye to our author for a while. In a conversation, a very serious conversation among three old men, our author had once written the sentence: "To be mistaken, and yet to go on believing in himself, that's what makes a man, and fame comes to him irrespective of triumph or defeat." From the perspective of the author, this sentence was a sort of anthropological elegy, a coded melancholy, but his critics saw it differently. They found the sentence alarming: a blank check, they said, for all kinds of political aberrations. At first the author didn't understand what his critics meant, but then he said to himself, all right, in the nineteenth century the sciences took on poetry, Nietzsche was opposed by theology; nowadays politics rears its head everywhere, all right, fine—blurred realm of shape-changing possibility—but all this together, the theoretical and the practical, caused the author to look about him, to see what other old and ancient people had done, and what age was, and what aging signified for an artist.

To get that out of the way first, my investigation did not concern itself with the physiology of aging. Medical literature on the subject is pretty scanty. Its current formula is that aging is not a process of being worn down or used up, but of adjusting, which I must say makes little sense to me. Further, it regrets the lack of scientific psychological investigations of the elderly (except in psychiatric institutions)—I wonder whether some of you might not regret that as well. Nor do I mean to speak of rejuvenation therapies, including the celebrated Bogomoletz serum. I do wonder, though, in what years aging actually begins.

The forty-six years at the end of which Schiller died, the forty-six years at the end of which Nietzsche fell silent, the forty-six years again at the end of which Shakespeare ceased his labors, to go on living in retirement for another five years; the thirty-six years after which Hölderlin fell ill—all this is no sort of age. But of course we are not really concerned with arithmetic here. There is little doubt that knowledge of an impending end may age an individual by decades. This will have been the case with the TB patients, with Schiller, therefore, Novalis, Chopin, Jens Peter Jacobsen, Mozart, and others. So far as the association is concerned between genius and an early death, which bourgeois-romantic ideology is so keen to promote, and likes to attribute to the voraciousness of art, we would have to look at it case by case. Some of those early deaths were actually from acute illnesses, as of typhoid: with Schubert and Büchner; of Raphael at thirty-seven of influenza, if we are to follow Vasari's account; through accident or war: Shelley, Byron, Franz Marc, Macke, Apollinaire, Heym, Lautréamont, Pushkin, Petöfi; by suicide: Kleist, Schumann, Van Gogh—in short, the ranks of those brought to a premature end by art alone are somewhat thinned.

Instead another, very curious consideration emerges when one looks at the dates. I share this with you not as a piece of profundity or metaphysics, but simply because it's interesting. This observation is: it is surprising, it is really quite remarkable how many old and very old individuals there are among figures of great renown. If we take the total figure that Kretschmer and Lange-Eichbaum gave for those who in the past four hundred years were accounted geniuses (or at least extremely talented), we arrive at a number in the order of one hundred and fifty or two hundred. It turns out that almost half these geniuses lived to an advanced age. Our traditionally allotted span is threescore and ten, so we won't look at that, but I should like to call your attention to the number of those who reached or exceeded seventy-five. I think you will be as surprised as I was. I will give you them now, in short order, the names and ages only, beginning with the painters and sculptors:

Titian 99, Michelangelo 89, Frans Hals 86, Goya 82, Hans Thoma 85, Liebermann 88, Munch 81, Degas 83, Bonnard 80, Maillol 83, Donatello 80, Tintoretto 76, Rodin 77, Käthe Kollwitz 78, Renoir 78, Monet 86, James Ensor 89, Menzel 90—and of those living: Matisse 84, Nolde 86, Gulbransson 81, Hofer and Scheibe both over 75, Klimsch 84.

And next the writers and poets: Goethe 83, Shaw 94, Hamsun 93, Maeterlinck 87, Tolstoy 82, Voltaire 84, Heinrich Mann 80, Ebner-Eschenbach 86, Pontoppidan 86, Heidenstam 81; Swift, Ibsen, Bjornsen, Rolland 78; Victor Hugo 83, Tennyson 83, Ricarda Huch 83, Hauptmann 84, Lagerlöf 82, Gide 82, Heyse 84, d'Annunzio 75; Spitteler, Fontane, Gustav Freytag 79; Frenssen 82—and among the living: Claudel 85; Thomas Mann, Hesse, Schröder, Döblin, Carossa, Dörffler all over 75; Emil Strauß 87.

Great old musicians are in shorter supply. I cite Verdi 88, Richard Strauss 85, Pfitzner 80, Heinrich Schütz 87, Monteverdi 76, Glück and Händel both 74, Bruckner 72, Palestrina 71, Buxtehude and Wagner both 70, Georg Schumann 81, Reznicek 85, Auber 84, Cherubini 82—and among the living: Sibelius 88.

My sampling is far from exhaustive; I did not proceed in any way systematically, I merely gathered up what presented itself to me in the course of my investigation, the lists could surely be extended. Now, one could attribute this to statistics—men are more apt to become great and famous if they have long lives and are able to remain productive for as long as possible. Even a biologistic account doesn't seem to me out of the question. Art is under one of its aspects a phenomenon of liberation and relaxation, of catharsis, and these have the closest ties to the organs. This thinking could be related to the Speranski theory, now making its way into pathology, that illness and potential illness tends to be much more governed by central impulses than had been thought hitherto, and that art is a central and primary impulse—of that there is surely no doubt. I am not making any very sweeping claim here, but a ripe old age seems even more noteworthy in view of the fact that we are talking about persons living at times when life expectancy was much shorter than today; you may know that the life expectancy of a newborn infant today is almost twice what it was in 1870.

The question of what aging means to an artist is a complex one, because subjective and objective meet there, with moods and crises on the one side, and history and description on the other. Never again to be able to attain a past mark, even if one struggles to over decades, say, as in the case of Swinburne: at twenty-nine he was an extraordinary force, then he went on writing and writing, and when he died at the age of seventy-two he was a fecund and pleasant versifier. One could say something similar about Hofmannsthal: the way from the poems of the twenty-year-old Loris to the political tangles of the *Tower* of the fifty-year-old was like the way from the feeding of the five thousand to a gathering of crumbs and leftovers. The cases of George and of Dehmel are similar. But all these are poets; in place of glimmer and suggestion of youth, you find application and force of will, but, as we know from Platen, "The runner will not catch the deer." From these introspectively colored hints I now turn to a perfectly concrete question, namely: What do art criticism and literary criticism actually mean by a work of old age, and how do they go about characterizing the changes from early work to an old style?

It's hard to gain any sort of coherent impression. A few authors see the issue in terms of such qualities as mildness, serenity, mercy, magnanimity, freedom from vanity in love and passion, while others like to adduce a quality of floating, drifting, a sense of already being in the beyond, and then the word "classical" turns up. Others again see the mood of old age as unsparingness, a radical honesty, putting one in mind of Shaw's saying that old men are dangerous because they don't care about the future. Pinder in his discussion of a painting by Frans Hals introduces a new quality again; he says the late style of an eighty-four-year-old is immediately detectable: only someone of such great age could represent such a petrified excess of experience and history, of explicit nearness to death. Petrified, he says, a contradiction of the previous notions of weightlessness, drift, and serenity. Another writes about Dürer: he died too soon, one would have wished his formal power to be softened by a mild and wide-ranging spirituality.—This is art criticism as a sort of requests program, where the listener calls in and asks for some mild and wide-ranging spirituality. Different again is Hausenstein on late Kubin. He says: "He is among those who in age come into not only superiority, but also an almost intoxicating fullness, where the effervescence and revolt of youth are revisited"—youth and age are entwined and twinned.

One more example from literature. In literature the word "late" is a very popular buzzword: late Rilke, late Hofmannsthal, late Eliot, late Gide—those are the essays one is forever coming across. I have in mind a book by a reputable literary historian who is discussing late Rilke. The book contains many profound and excellent remarks, but its argument is more or less as follows: phase 1: stage of experimentation, drafts, beginnings, followed by phase 2: of "entire being" and "inherent form." Only in phase 2 did Rilke become "what he thought he was all along, but wasn't." So, "inherent"—what does that mean? For me the word is too stuffed with eschatology, and ideology, and old-fashioned developmental theory. Our literary historian sees his Rilke as striving for some ideal state—which is "inherently" his, the author's, ideal state—but this seems to me all the more inapplicable to Rilke, since his early phase brought out poems of such flawless beauty that no "inherently" can dim them. I sometimes think the compulsion to view an artist in phases is specifically German in its unabashed idealism.

One of the most important books on our subject is [Albert Erich] Brinckmann's *Late Works by Great Masters*. Brinckmann approaches the intellectual changes in creative persons with his own antithesis: opposition and melting are his two crampons. Opposition, the first stage, the glimpsing and representation of relations between people, actions, the objects in a room, colors— and then there is the subsequent stage of melting, where the colors are diffused into one overall tonality, the elements, previously juxtaposed and contrasted, are shown in an overall setting, often melting into something unspecified. Then Brinckmann talks about "forsaking a state of tension in the interests of a higher freedom"—wherever the word "freedom" crops up, he gets a little unclear, and I can follow him only reluctantly. But Brinckmann performs quite compellingly his analysis of several painters who tackled a subject once in their youth, and then again in their age. He fixes the climacteric of productive structure in the thirty-fifth and the sixtieth year, claiming in this to follow Freud. And it is following Freud too that Brinckmann— uniquely—ponders the relation between sexuality and artistic production. Even though the theme is something of a digression at this point in my talk, let me at least mention it. The relation is certainly real, but it is quite opaque. You will be familiar with the great number of famous homosexual writers and artists in whose work their orientation is not made apparent. If you name the four greatest figures in Western culture—Plato, Michelangelo, Shakespeare, and Goethe—then two were notoriously homosexual, one of uncertain orientation, and only Goethe seems to have been straightforwardly orthodox. Then there are the sexless geniuses: you will recall the famous testament of Adolf Menzel, from which it appears that not once in ninety years of life did he have congress with a woman. The question of the connection between failing sexuality and fading production is for now impossible to answer. You know Goethe at seventy-five fell in love with Ulrike and wanted to marry her, and in Gide's *Diaries* we come across the following almost grotesque situation: in Tunis, at the age of seventy-two, he falls in love with a fifteen-year-old Arab boy, and describes intoxicating nights reminiscent of the headiest years of his youth. It stretches credulity, his rapt recording that the first time he clapped eyes on the boy, who was working in his hotel as a page, he felt so shy and delicate that he did not dare to approach him—Gide aged seventy-two in the Gretchen role. It's a fascinating theme, but whether the dimming of eros lames the intellect or, as some say, lends it wings is not a question that can be settled by our existing methodologies.

A special case that repeatedly took my attention was Michelangelo—the Pietà Rondanini, which he created at the age of eighty-nine but never completed. This Pietà is the subject of such wildly divergent views from important critics that there is nothing but to conclude that a radical change of structure must have been involved in the artist. One author writes of a new peak of inwardness and spirituality. A second has it that a degree of emotion emanates from this work that will not be gainsaid, something ethereally spiritual, a floating in which one last sigh is paired with the first glimmer of coming release. But the other side says that in this work he turns his back on the glories of his youth; Simmel goes so far as to claim: "Michelangelo has here denied the life principle of his art. This is his most traitorous and tragic work, the seal on his inability through art, through the sensual contemplation of centered creation to attain release—the last shattering calamity of his life." Here, then, one has little alternative but to suppose, is an instance of a great man unable to go on using his established methods and techniques—presumably because they will have struck him as outmoded and conventional—but with no expressive forms available for his new contents, breaking off, and lowering his hands. Perhaps an instance of those weighty words in Malraux's *Psychology of Art*: "First they invent a language, then they learn to speak it, often inventing another one in the process. When the style of death touches them, they remember how in their youth they broke with their teachers, and then they break with their own work." Malraux goes on to say: "The highest embodiment of an artist is founded equally on the renunciation of his masters and the destruction of everything he himself once was." These are grave words, and we apply them to a man whose shoulders supported almost an entire century, and whose fame is one of the meridians of our planet.

At the end of this part of my talk, I want to mention a book that threw up a new question to me in my investigations. It is Riezler's book on Beethoven, the last chapter of which is called "The Last Style." The description of this last style is gorgeous, persuasive, and dictated by eminently superior understanding. But, I said to myself, it remains a fact that the author has had to translate his musical impressions and his compositional analyses into the medium of language, and to express something in words that music by its nature does not contain. When I look at the words used to depict the incarnation of this last style, I find: "force," "monumentality," "gigantism," "tectonically anchored," but also: "free-floating," "serene," "ethereal," "ultimate spirituality"—words, then, from the same impressionistic register we found in the analyses of the painters' late works, and which one might presumably find occasionally in descriptions of the great works of younger artists as well. At the beginning of this last chapter, Riezler offers his conviction that the description of a characteristic late style must be possible in every century and every medium, since "the universal-artistic anticipates and preempts the formal variations of the different arts." But how should one think of this universal-artistic? What sort of ultimative hieroglyph is it? Couldn't one equally well argue that outside of music, painting, and poetry there is a linguistic means that serves the understanding, and from which our various system-mongers seek to draw their attempted characterizations?

At this juncture I asked myself, what do aging and being old actually look like to the artist himself? Take Flaubert—sitting in his narrow house in Rouen, in his room that he doesn't leave for days on end, night after night the light from his windows shines out over the river, so that the bargemen on the Seine use it as an aid to navigation. He is fifty-nine, no great age, but he's used up, he has deep bags under his eyes, his lids are wrinkled with scorn, scorn for this *gent épicière*, those grocers, those middle classes—yes, the court has allowed that his descriptions in *Bovary* are not immoral, but it has recommended that he use his gifts of observation on more sympathetic beings, to show off better hearts—then he showed better hearts—and when *Sentimental Education* appeared, they wrote: a cretin, a pimp, he dirties the gutter water in which he washes.

In his youth he wrote: if one wants to create something lasting, one must not scoff at fame—but look at him later, what was there that he did not laugh at, and himself most of all, he was incapable of seeing himself shaving in the mirror without laughing out loud—now he drew up a list of the idiocies of the dead whose names represented humanity. Change the record? Once more to sit in the bistro down in the town, in that state of concentration, in that constant visual and acoustic alertness, to penetrate the object, to go behind the faces, to make once more that tragic, superhuman effort of observation, of finding expressions, of collecting sentences that work—there they are sitting at the bar, all of them after money, all of them after love, and he is in quest of expression, of a sequence of sentences, these two worlds must embrace one another—another record?—realism, artistry, psychology—they call me cold, being cold isn't so bad, I'd rather be cold than sing and interpret, for whom, for what— do you believe anything, Flaubert, say yes or no—yes, I believe that belief is only to have been constituted in such and such a way as to assume this or that—no, I don't believe, *je suis mystique et je ne crois à rien.*

That's the old Flaubert.

Then there's Leonardo in the little Château Ducloux [Manoir du Cloux] on the Loire, Italy is off-limits to him, his patrons there are either dead or locked up. What does he think about in his evenings, the king is hunting, silence, only the metal tolling of the bells in their clock tower and the cries of the wild swans on the water, the river that is lined with poplars, so that it reminds him of Lombardy. The king has offered him 4,000 gulden for the *Gioconda*, but he won't part with her, the king insists, the old man throws himself at his feet, weeps, makes a spectacle of himself in front of the guests, he offers him his latest picture instead, it's a *John the Baptist,* but not the *Gioconda,* no, she's as dear to him as life itself. He took five years over her, hunched, silent, aging, not showing her to anyone. In the room where he painted, full of torsos of Hellenic statues, dog-headed Egyptian divinities in black granite, stones of the gnostics with runic inscriptions, Byzantine parchments gone hard as ivory, with scraps of lost Greek verses, potsherds with Assyrian wedge script, writings of the Persian mages bound in iron, papyri from Memphis, diaphanous and flower-petal fine: that was where he had to change, yearn, perhaps find himself wanting, he lived five years thrown back on his innermost self. To the king and the court he was a pathetic figure, but that was how he got to keep the painting in his room. The winding staircase was narrow and steep, he had fits of dizziness and breathlessness when he climbed it, then his right side was lamed, he could still draw with his left hand, but not paint, in his evenings he played cards and games with wooden splinters with a monk, then his left side went lame; he had just said pick yourself up and throw yourself into the sea, when he died, and now he was at rest like a fallen weight. After his death, a Russian icon painter who lived nearby approached the easel with his *John the Baptist,* and said: Shameless, who is this scruffy fellow stripped like a harlot with neither beard nor mustache, no forerunner of Christ! Devil stuff, don't sully my eyes!

That was the old da Vinci.

The evenings of those lives! Most of them in poverty, coughing, bad backs, addicts, drinkers, a few criminals, almost all of them unmarried, almost all of them childless, that bio-negative

Olympiad, European Olympiad, cisatlantic Olympiad, bearing the grandeur and misery of postclassical man for four centuries. Whoever was born in favorable circumstances might wind up with a house, like Goethe or Rubens; whoever was in straitened circumstances painted every day of his life without a penny in his pocket, wavy olive groves, and if he lives in the Space Age he looks out of a back room at a rabbit run and a couple of hydrangea bushes. If you look at them all, there's really only one thing you can say: they were all compulsives. "I go on trembling like the snake in the hand of the tamer until I go cold. Everything good I ever did came about in that way," said Delacroix, and Beckmann wrote: "I would live in sewers and crawl through pipes so long as I could paint." Snakes, sewers, pipes—such are the preludes to the evenings of those lives.

Now please don't accuse me of dwelling on the macabre, and of foisting my out-of-date perspectives from the time of the *poètes maudits* on you. The psychopathologies and sociological analyses of the lives and the evenings of the lives of these highly gifted individuals are not by me, they're by others. Such thoughts and visions may be a little alarming in our time, where the artist has taken on something of the appearance of the bourgeois, and passes himself off as a sort of official, perhaps even feels that's what he is, a functionary in a certain position that pushes him toward material security and state commissions. The presence of so much routine criticism, reviews of exhibitions and books assigned and paid for in the press, has had the effect of seeming to draw him into the general mishmash where the individualism of the epoch ends. But don't be deceived, the collective corrective doesn't really touch this compulsive, who continues to mount his poison green helicopter into his esoteric studio. It's not so long ago that the eighty-three-year-old Degas said: "A painting is something that takes as much cunning and wickedness as a crime—forgery and add a shot of nature."

The poison green helicopter may be a touch banal, but let's get on board anyway for a moment, to look down on what people can't take with them of the world.

Much affection for humankind isn't included. Do you recall a self-portrait of Tintoretto's, an old man, I don't know where the original is, I saw it only in reproduction, but there's just one word for it: rancid.* Or Rembrandt's late self-portrait: averted, cautious, a chilly count-me-out. None of the great old ones was an idealist, they got by without idealism, they knew and wanted what was possible—it's only the dilettantes who like to enthuse and rave.

Art—these people say—art must bring the relation between the world and the absolute into focus. Art must restore the center without losing the background. Art must show man as the image of God—now is there anything that isn't the image of God, I'd be surprised, I wouldn't even exclude the tiger—because art doesn't "have to" do anything at all. The helicopter has a radio on board, it's just playing a hit song from the film *Moulin Rouge*, the tune makes me tremble: under certain circumstances a good pop song can contain more for the ages than a motet, and a word can weigh heavier than a victory.

* This is surely the *White-Bearded Man* of 1545, which hangs in the Kunsthistorisches Museum in Vienna. It is near the center of Thomas Bernhard's 1985 novel *Old Masters*, to which Benn's word "rancid" is, in the best sense, applicable.

Those oldsters! What I see is less something high-flying than the century and compulsion. A rosy century—fine, we paint bucolic scenes, especially the middle, but what do we paint in a black century? Perhaps something technical for the conference market? Technology is a favorite topic, and people say it's important to integrate it. Everything has to harmonize: the lyric poem and the Geiger counter, inoculations and Church Fathers—mind you, leave nothing out, otherwise the spirit of global coalition is threatened. Even language has to take it on board, which is an idea that would never have occurred to me. A powerful and organic language lives out of itself, reproduces out of itself; it absorbs but, thanks to its immanent law, integrates a few tags from physics and mechanics, those pathetic scraps, they are left to heal into the body of the language without troubling its transcendence.

Gaining altitude now—the earth is disappearing from sight, but we can still see its colossal complexes, its depots, its so-called institutions. I too wandered through them, as one of my oldsters would put it today. I suffered from depression, I went to an institute, and was referred to a psychoanalyst. He said you are missing oral-narcissistic gratification—you are introverted, you understand! I replied that "introverted" and "extroverted" both struck me as rather crude concepts: people suffer to a greater or lesser extent, are more or less free, and of the two the more free seem more chained to me. Contact insufficiency, said the therapist, pushing a brochure, "Your Libido and You," into my hands, and then he lapsed back into his trance.

Then I had heard, one of my old men would say today, that thinking sets you free, thinking makes you happy, so I set foot in a few more institutes and turned to the thinkers in them. But sociology, phenomenology, foundation theory (doesn't it all sound like Puccini?), ontology—where is existence anyway, outside of my pictures, and why do people keep going on about things?—things occur when you allow them, formulate them, paint them; if you don't admit them, they have no existence. These thinkers with their foundation of being, which no one can actually see, completely formless, all of them are just contributions, contributioneers is what they are—they turn on the tap, usually a bit of Plato comes out, and they splash about in that for a while, and then the next one comes along for the bathroom. No one accomplishes anything, I need to finish my own stuff myself. All of them are idealists, things really start there, all of them optimists, at the age of seventy-five they order a new jerkin for themselves. Schopenhauer was, so far as I know, comfortably off, of independent means, and still he thought he thought interestingly, vigorously, and sublimely, surely no gentleman nowadays thinks anymore—the only exception might be Wittgenstein, who says, "The limits of my language mean the limits of my world" and "What the picture shows is its meaning." That's healthy thinking, concrete thinking, with no dangly coats being trailed; that's deliberate self-limiting to the linking of protocol sentences—that's picturesque thinking, Lethe, here endeth the myth.

So how is the situation? Desperate! Give me libidinal supplements and a secure pre-Spenglerian culture circle. Space exploration is not yet so advanced that we could reach the stars and rethink. Oh, why was I not a landscape describer, professionally, from the Teutoburg Forest to Astrakhan, all done by Volkswagen today, with the forest floor under my feet?

Nations are queer things, the old man continues to think. They would like to have some interesting minds, but they insist on defining what's interesting and what isn't. They want names of international renown, but whoever attacks the nation's predilections is ruled out. They want to be delivered of universal works, but they draw up the roster of midwives and furnish them with manuals on accouchement. *Penthesilea* would never have been written if it had come to a vote; Strindberg, Nietzsche, El Greco never appeared. But conformism would always have been Johnny-on-the-spot, and he always was there, only he isn't responsible for four hundred years of Western art. The writers have often envied the painters, they can paint oranges and asphodels and jugs, even lobsters and crustaceans, and no one holds it against them that they failed to weave in the problem of social housing; in everything written the union has rights— "antisocial," that's the word, and "art must." It's probably futile to point out that Flaubert was chronicling the painful position of oppressed artists who couldn't do everything they wanted and felt, but only what was given to them within the limits of their language and style.

Seventy-three hundred meters above sea level—that's the death line—another kilometer and we're there. The passengers look down. When the diamond merchant Salomon Rosbach leapt from the Empire State Building, he left an enigmatic message: "No more up, no more down, I'm jumping." A good message, says the passenger, no up, no down, the center is damaged, needle and compass are askew, but the species is thriving and taking the tablets. The body has gotten more morbid, modern medicine is pointing it in the direction of a thousand and one diseases, they duly break out in it with scientific rigor—not a word against practitioners of course, great people; earlier, when you got a mosquito bite, you scratched the place, now they can prescribe a dozen salves for it and none of them are of the least use, but, hey, that's life, and that's progress. Bodies have gotten more morbid, but they live longer. A Roman in the days of the empire made it to twenty-five, but he was carried by Roman *virtus*; today people are soft with prophylactics, and can barely make it home after so many batteries of tests.

Brains live longer, but where there was once stay and resistance, they now develop bare patches—or when you look out of your window down at the ground, can you imagine a God who made something so mild as plants and trees? Rats, pestilence, noise, despair, yes, but flowers? There is a fourteenth-century painting, *Creation of the Plants*, where you see a little crooked black-bearded god raising a disproportionately large right hand as though he were using it to pull two flanking trees out of the ground, but other than them, everything still looks fairly barren—can you imagine this friendly creator today? Vices, worms, maggots, sloths, and skunks—yes, masses of them all the time, in fresh consignments, 100 percent new and improved—but a tender little God raising a couple of trees? No trees, no flowers, but robotic brains, artificial insemination of cows and women, chicken farms with piped music to lay by, artificial redoubling of chromosomes to aid the creation of giant bastard forms—air too cold, heat too hot, you inject a seed—run away quickly before he shoots you in the leg.

There at last. The old man enters his studio, a bare room with a big table, covered with notes and scraps of paper. He goes up to it: what shall I do today, essay, poem, dialogue—the simultaneous emergence of form and content is another philosophical illusion—I could use this bit here or there, I dye, I knit together, I plumb in, everything happens the way I want it, I strode through my beginning, I stride through my end, Moira, the part allotted to me—only one thing is certain: when something is finished, it must be complete—and then what?

Take another look at them, the most famous works of old age: what do they mean? For instance the "novella": a menagerie catches fire, the cages burn down, the tigers break out, the lions are loose, and everything transpires in harmony—no, this earth is burned, scalped by lightning, today the tigers are biting. Or what is it with *Faust, Part Two*? Surely the most mysterious present of Germany's to the peoples of the world, but all those choirs, those gryphons, lamias, pulcinellas, ants, cranes, and *empusae*, all of it buzzing and droning away to itself warbling up to the circles of the elves and the stars and the blessed boys. Where does it all come from, it's fantasy, table-tipping, telepathy, eccentricities, there's someone standing on a balcony, unreal and immobile, blowing light- or dark-colored soap bubbles, conjuring up more and more clay pipes and straws to blow more and more bubbles—a splendid balcony god, antiquity and baroque still instinct in him, wonders and secrets about his loins, but nowadays one watches more or less dry-eyed. It's all so many metaphors.

Translators and explicators will continue to circle round the very greatest for another couple of centuries, but before long no one will understand their language anymore—then what? Primitivism, archaism, classicism, mannerism, abstraction, in a word, the Quaternary, then what? The rooms, the correspondences, the feelings they have thrown open are too cavernous, too numerous, too heavy—perhaps the creation of art is a shallow reaction, maybe suffering silently on the human surface is . . . deeper? What did Jehovah put in our nature, what did he refer us to: creative release or the immovable place, the Bo tree, under which we will silently encounter Kama-Mara, the god of love and death? How many hours of my life have I spent over the sentence of the balcony god, twisting and turning it, listen to it: "At its highest peak, poetry seems to be perfectly external. The more it recedes into the interior, the more it sinks away."— What does that mean? So I must deny my inner self, bamboozle it, play tricks on it—is that the prerequisite for poetry? What is poetry then? Conjuring, rope trick, nothing, and a spot of varnish? And from the East I heard the same tune, Master Kung Tsi, saying, "The painter in whom significance preponderates over line is coarse"—so for him as well, the higher, the manipulated, the confected is the style. But when Guardini says, "Behind each work of art there is a wide open space"—what is it that opens, since we're meant to brush everything out, and cover it over?—or when a great philosopher writes that art is "the getting to work of truth," what truth does he mean, a truth of making, of sketches and cartoons, or is truth perhaps only mentioned so that philosophy can stick its nose in, because art isn't to do with truth, but expression? But, last question, what is it with this expression clustered over the deeps—is it expression's fault? It could be.

Probably I'm too old to get to the bottom of all this, tiredness and melancholy fog my brain. I have heard Pablo de Sarasate on the violin and Caruso in the Met. The Astors were sitting in the diamond horseshoe. I have seen Bergmann operate, and paraded in front of the last Kaiser. I learned to read by the light of an oil lamp, and studied Haeckel's forbidden *Riddles of the World.* I have driven and flown, but I have also seen clipper ships and skies without vapor trails—past—gone. And if I say today that it was all more laden than it seemed, everything more predestined than it gave the appearance of being, and, strangest of all, one was much more in the air than one thought in one's seeming autonomy. In instance of this: there were painters who all their lives painted in silver, one of them, or in yellow, or another in brown, and there was a generation whose poetry was mostly nouns. Not a literary gag, it was in the air, in the air put together from heterogeneous elements. I lately read the following story about Clémenceau. He had taken on a new personal secretary, and was informing him of his duties on the first day. Some letters, Clémenceau said, you will have to write by yourself. Listen: "A sentence consists of a noun and a verb—if you want to use an adjective as well, get my permission first." Get my permission first! It's the same as what Carl Sternheim told me when we were both young: he said, when you've written something, look it over again, and cut out the adjectives, then your meaning will be clearer. That turned out to be right, it was the compulsory check for my generation, the leaving out of the sprawling, explaining adjectives.

My generation! But now the next is already at hand, the young people, our youth! God preserve their desire to copy us, it'll go away after a time by itself. But when they produce a new style—*evoe!* A new style is a new person. Genetics has brought forth little that is not tangled, but one thing seems to be there: a new generation means a new brain, and a new brain is a new reality and fresh neuroses, and the name of the whole thing is evolution, and so the culture circle keeps turning. If I had anything to give this youth from my pulpit of age, then it would include the following: if you've published four rhymed or unrhymed poems, or have managed to sketch a recognizable goat, then don't expect the Lord Mayor to telephone you on your birthday, after all, you're just doing something human. Perhaps you should remember instead that in his twenty-ninth year Schubert was urged to buy unlined manuscript paper—and draw in the lines himself, it was cheaper. Of course people say all sorts of things, but it still applies, not everyone is so advanced that by the age of thirty-one he no longer needs to economize.

Followers, successors, I don't mind if you're provoked by me, I hope it makes you tough. Toughness is the best gift for the artist, toughness against yourself and your work. What did Thomas Mann say? "Sooner spoil a work than not go as far as you can at every point of it." Or as I tried to put it earlier, one thing is for certain: if something is finished, it must be complete. Don't for one moment forget the dubiousness and eccentricity of your enterprise, the dangers and hatreds that attend your activity. Keep in mind that coldness and egoism are part of your task. Your work has left behind the temples and the sacrificial vessels and the painting of pillars, the painting of chapels is no longer part of it either. You are wallpapering with yourself, and you have no alternative. Don't allow yourself to be seduced by comfort—a book is 312 pages, and retails at 13.80 deutsche marks in hardback. There is no restoration. Intellectual things are irreversible, you must pursue your path to the end, to the end of the night. With your back to the wall, in the wretchedness of fatigue, in the gray of emptiness, you will read your Job and your Jeremiah, and you will stick it out. Draft your propositions as harshly as you can, because when the epoch draws to a close and kills your song, you will be measured by your sentences. What you don't write will not exist. You will make enemies, be alone, a nutshell on the sea, a walnut shell emitting odd clanking noises, rattling with cold, trembling with your own revulsion at yourself, but don't put out an SOS—in the first place, no one will hear you, and in the second, your ending will be peaceful after so much travail.

Ladies and gentlemen, the portrait of age is done, we have left the studio, the helicopter is sinking back to earth—there are many questions left unanswered, or even unasked. As, for instance: should one repudiate the work of one's youth, or retouch it, adapt it to a different internal situation (if you happen to have one), should you turn yourself into an old gazelle when you were a young jackal . . . but it's too late to think about that, our vessel is landing. An *homme du monde* climbs out of the gondola; with gray tie and black Homburg hat, he disappears into the bustle of the airport. The airport is in the country, the gentleman strolls to its periphery, where he sees poplars, as in the Loire valley, and as once in Lombardy, and there is a ribboning river like the Seine, where the mariners look up at night to his light. The same things return eternally, as long as there is any resemblance. And when nothing any longer resembles anything, and the great rules are interchangeable—they will still create some semblance of order.

"To be mistaken, and yet to go on believing in himself, that's what makes a man, and fame comes to him irrespective of triumph or defeat"—yes, he would write that sentence again, if he were to start over—even if it led astray, even if it distorted—what sentence of understanding is without blame? I have worked, in the light of the West, I lived as if the day were there, my day. I was the one I shall have been. And that's why at the end I appeal to the Church Fathers, the old ones, the ones many hundreds of years old, and say: *non confundar in aeternum.* I too shall not be condemned in eternity.

# *thanks and acknowledgments*

I owe thanks, once again, to Jonathan Galassi for the trust—impulsive to begin with, then steady and unfazed—that he brought to this project, from the moment I first took it to him in 2005; he contrived to give me the feeling that whatever I came up with (and wherever and whenever), he would be ready for it: an extraordinary sense to get from a publisher.

One of the pleasant aspects of something long-running as this has been is it gives one a dependable subject of conversation with friends; Jonathan Aaron, Durs Grünbein, Lawrence Joseph, Paul Keegan, and Jamie McKendrick were all good enough to bandy Benn with me for many hours.

Extravagant thanks—really *outré* thanks—to the princes who edit *Poetry* and *The Times Literary Supplement* for giving Benn house room ("a house is not an inn") in their journals. The book is dedicated to them.

Some of the individual poems and prose pieces first appeared as follows, sometimes in (something I have wanted to say for years!) slightly different versions:

*Twentieth-Century German Poetry* (New York: Farrar, Straus and Giroux, 2006): "Night Café," "*Par ci, par là*," and "Listen:"
*The New Republic*: "Silence"
*The New York Review of Books*: "Herr Wehner"
*The Paris Review*: "Circulation," "Songs," "Never Lonelier," "Despair," and "Rowans"

*Poetry*: "Can Be No Sorrow," "Little Aster," "Beautiful Youth,"
"Alaska," "The Young Hebbel," "Threat," "Express Train,"
"Caryatid," "Jena," "Asters," "Tracing," "Static Poems,"
"Evenings of Certain Lives," "A Shadow on the Wall," "Frag-
ments," "Think of the Unsatisfied Ones," "Syntax," "Finis Polo-
niae," "Gladioli," "Restaurant," "Theoretical Afterlife?," "Still
Life," "Hymn," "What's Bad," "Impromptu," "Left the House,"
"People Met," "Last Spring," "Late (V)," "They Are Human Af-
ter All," "No Tears," "Divergences," "Zeh was a pharmacist . . . ,"
"Radio," and "Fragments 1953"

*The Poetry Book Society Anthology 3*, ed. William Scammell (Lon-
don: Hutchinson, 1992): "Chopin"

*The Threepenny Review*: "The Season"

*The Times Literary Supplement*: "Englisches Café," "Death of
Orpheus," "Nocturne," "Blue Hour," "Encounters," "Bauxite,"
"Late," "Devastations," "1886," "Wet Fences," "Little Sweet
Face," and "How are the beech trees in September . . ."

# index of poem titles and first lines in german

# index of poem titles and first lines in english